Editor
Ev Stanton, M.A.

Editorial Project Manager
Mara Ellen Guckian

Illustrator
Kelly McMahon

Cover Artist
Denise Bauer

Editors in Chief
Karen J. Goldfluss, M.S. Ed.
Ina Massler Levin, M.A.

Art Production Manager
Kevin Barnes

Art Coordinator
Renée Christine Yates

Imaging
Ev Stanton, M.A.
James Edward Grace
Craig Gunnell

Publisher
Mary D. Smith, M.S. Ed.

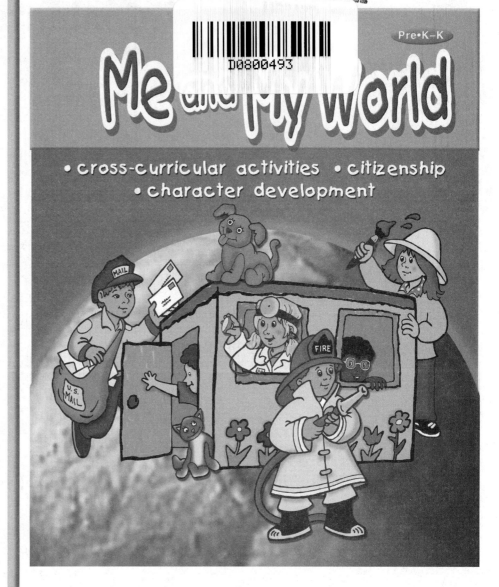

Me and My World

• cross-curricular activities • citizenship
• character development

Pre•K–K

Author
Tracy Edmunds, M.A.

Teacher Created Resources, Inc.
6421 Industry Way
Westminster, CA 92683
www.teachercreated.com

ISBN: 978-1-4206-9269-3

© 2008 Teacher Created Resources, Inc.

Made in U.S.A.

Teacher Created Resources

Table of Contents

Introduction

Social studies (the study of people and their relationships to each other and to their environments) is a natural part of early childhood education. Very young children are focused on their own wants and needs. As they reach school age they become developmentally ready to begin forming relationships outside of their own families and exploring the world around them. Preschool and kindergarten classrooms are perfect settings for young children to begin expanding their experiences with other people and with their communities.

Me and My World is full of engaging cross-curricular activities designed to expand a child's view from self to family, to community, to world. Character development and citizenship are woven through each unit. The units in this book build upon one another—children first focus on what they know and what they are able to do in the "Me" unit. They then gradually expand their awareness of the world around them and their place in it in the "My Family," "My Classroom Community," and "My World" units. The activities in this book will help young children move beyond their natural egocentricity and begin to take on the perspective of others, becoming active participants in the classroom community and the larger world beyond.

Character Education Traits—Pieces of the Puzzle

By helping students become productive and responsible members of their families, their classrooms, and their communities, early childhood education prepares students for life. Throughout this book, you will find puzzle pieces indicating the traits of good character that are addressed in the lessons:

Citizenship
Cooperation
Courage
Empathy
Fairness
Integrity
Kindness
Perseverance
Respect
Responsibility
Self-discipline

By helping children acquire and fit together these "pieces of the puzzle," teachers will guide them on their first steps toward responsible adulthood.

Social Studies Themes

The following social studies themes are addressed throughout the units, as indicated by a globe icon:

- Identity
- Culture
- Time
- Geography

- Civics
- Relationships
- Economics
- Environments

My Body

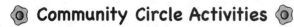

◉ Community Circle Activities ◉

Identity

Myself

Young children have naturally narrow world views. Their world is small and they are focused mainly on themselves. The activities in this chapter take advantage of children's natural curiosity about their own bodies and what makes them unique as a starting point for learning about the people around them.

Getting to Know Me

Place a full-length mirror in front of the group. Ask each child to stand in front of it and look at himself or herself for a moment, then close his or her eyes and describe what he or she saw (*"I have black hair and brown eyes. My shirt is red. I have freckles on my nose."*). Other students can add to the descriptions. See how detailed students can get!

You will need a full-length mirror for this activity.

Name That Part

Practice naming the parts of the body. Cut out and laminate the Body Parts Cards on pages 5–12. Hold up each card and ask students to touch that body part on their bodies and say its name. Ask students to tell what they can do with that body part (*"I can see with my eyes." "I can kick a ball with my foot."*)

Cut out and laminate the Body Parts Cards on pages 5–12.

Move It!

Cut out and assemble the Movement Cube on page 14. Have a student roll the die, then have everyone do the movement together. Use the blank on page 15 to create a different cube.

Cut out and assemble the Movement Cube on page 14 or 15.

Musical Bodies

Do "The Hokey Pokey," and sing "Head, Shoulders, Knees, and Toes" to practice naming body parts.

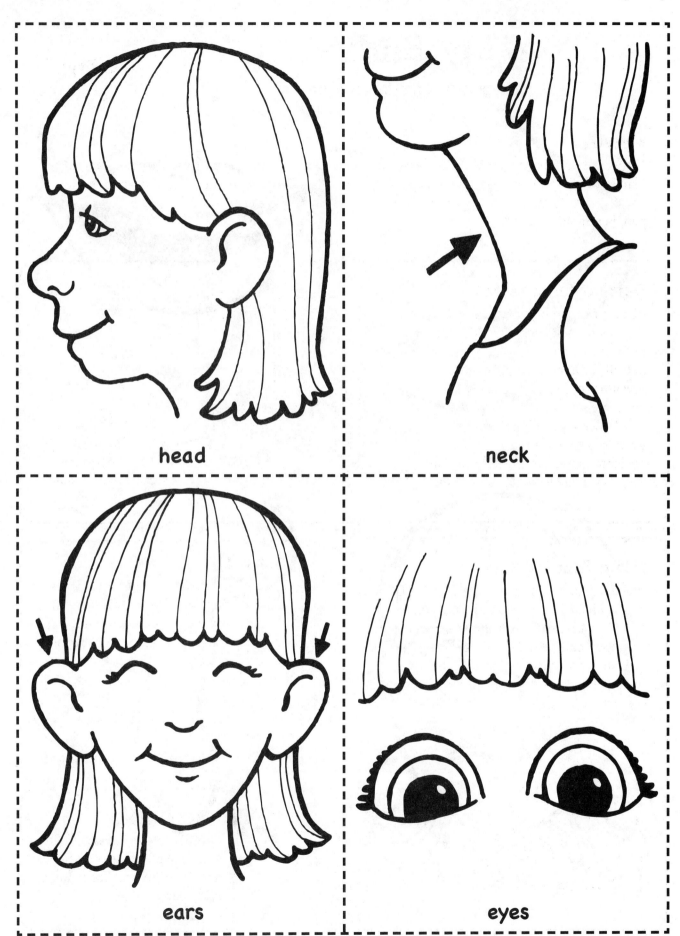

head

neck

ears

eyes

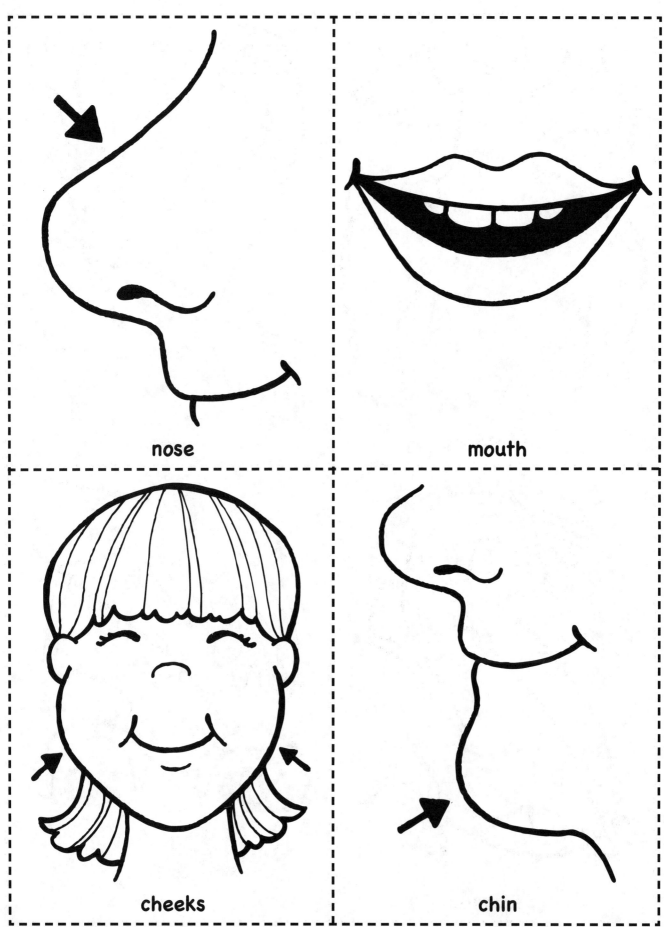

nose

mouth

cheeks

chin

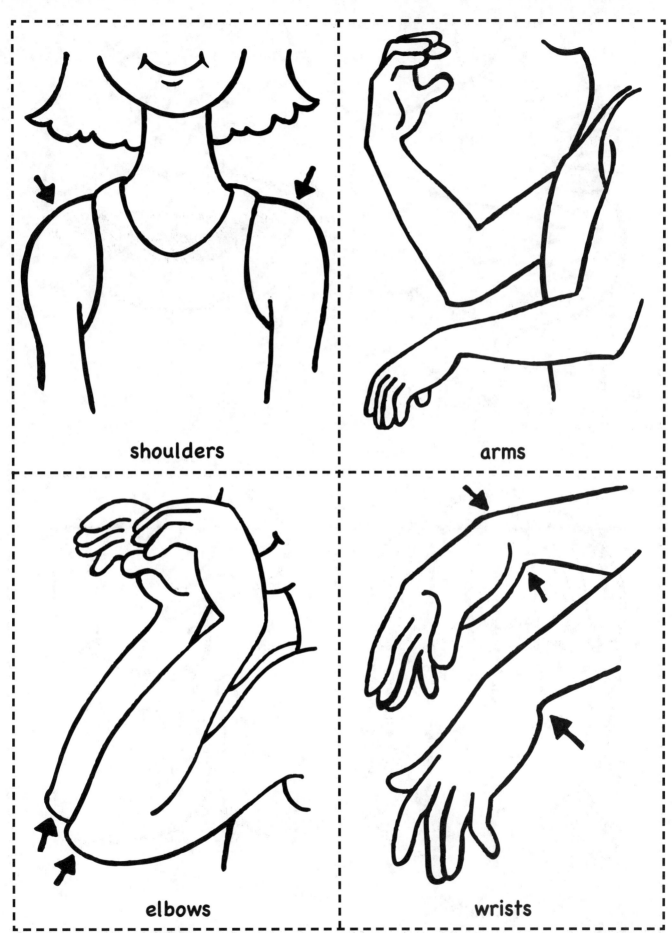

shoulders

arms

elbows

wrists

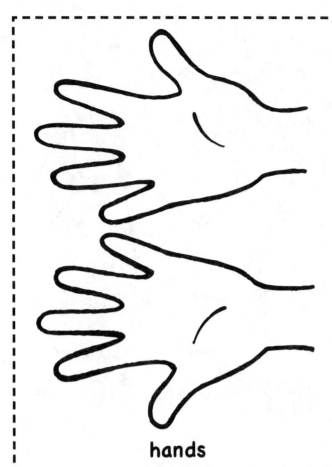

hands

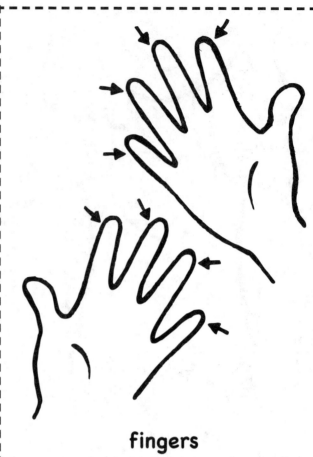

fingers

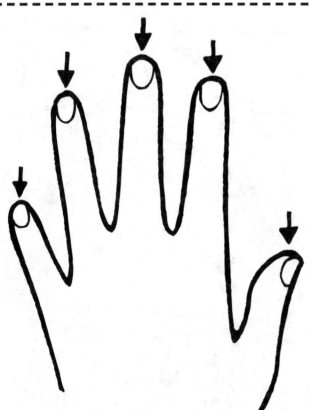

fingernails

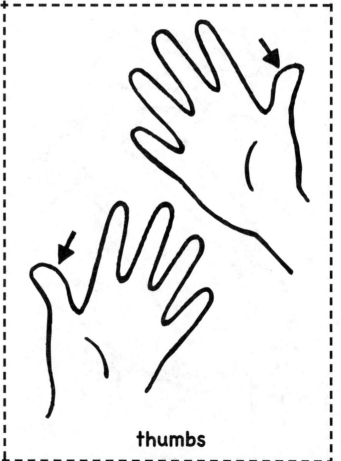

thumbs

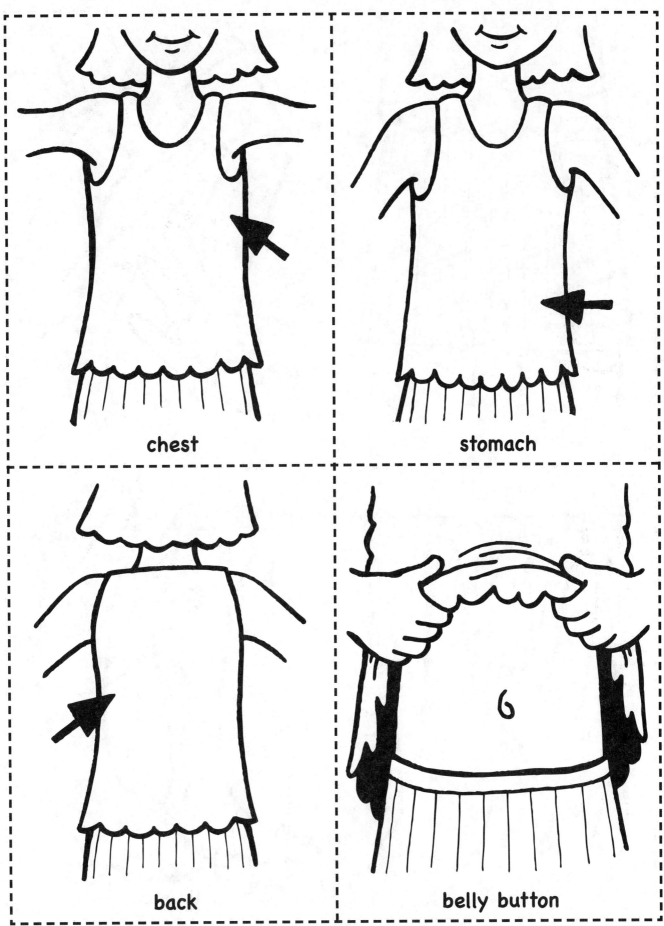

chest

stomach

back

belly button

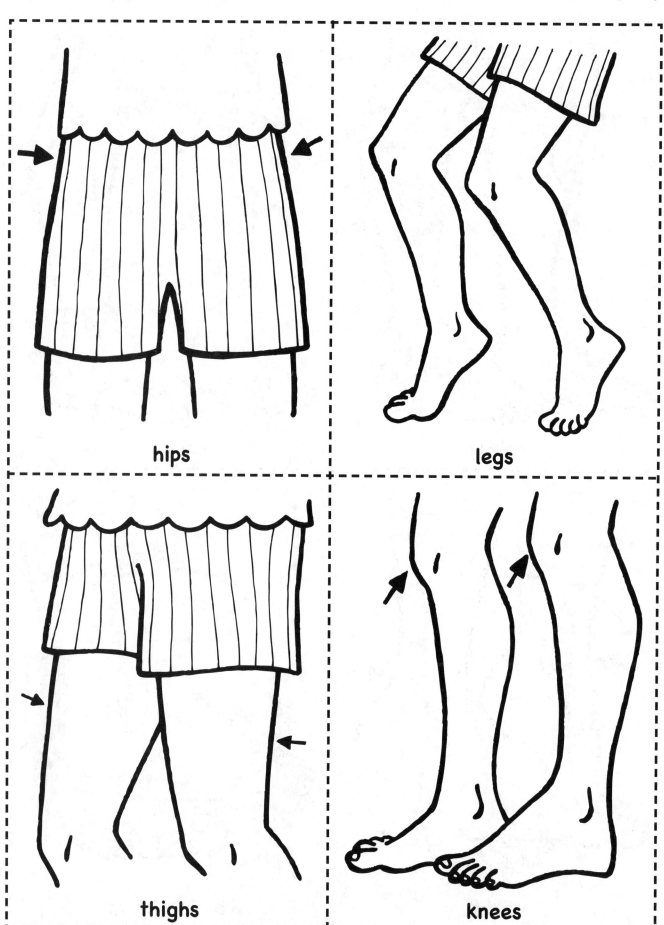

hips

legs

thighs

knees

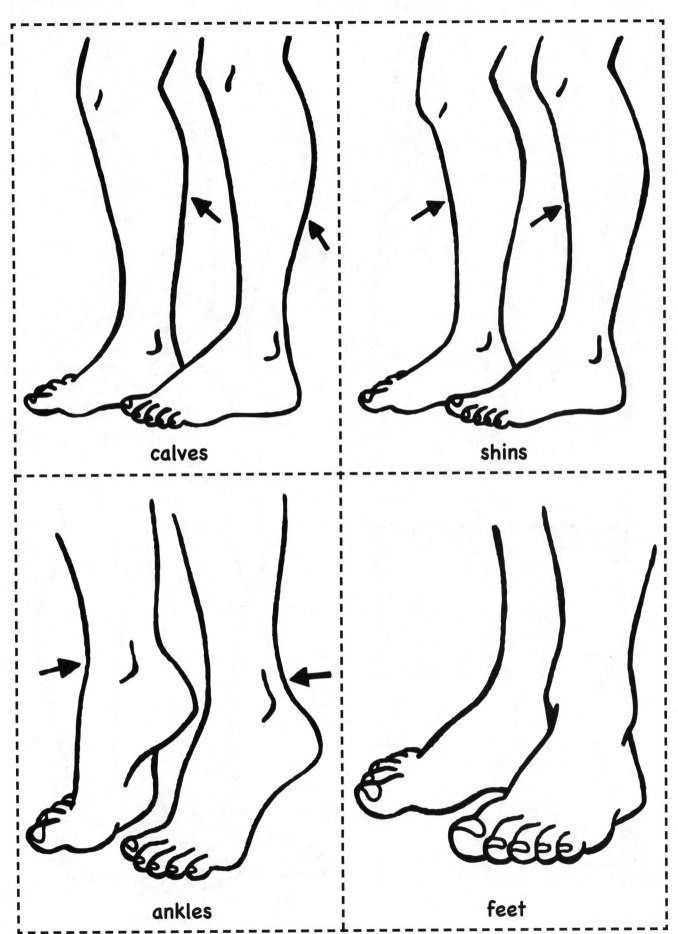

calves

shins

ankles

feet

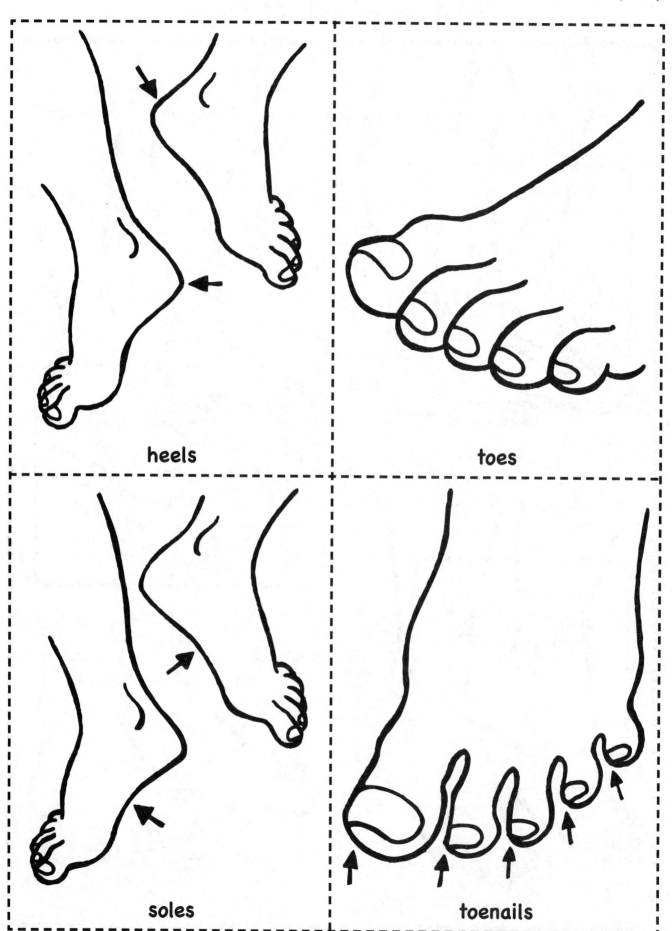

heels

toes

soles

toenails

Movement Cubes

Step 1

Copy the die pattern onto cardstock. Color and decorate the die. Cut out the die along the solid lines.

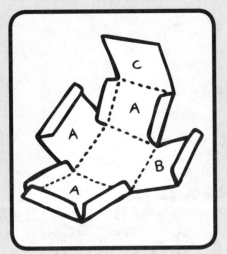

Step 2

Fold the die pattern along all the dotted lines. Flip the shape over so the decorated side is facing away from you.

Step 3

Bend up the sides labeled "A," and apply glue on the two tabs where shown. Fold up the side labeled "B," and press "B" against the glue-covered tabs.

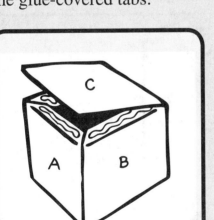

Step 4

Put some glue on all remaining tabs. Fold side "C" over the top of the die and press against the glue-covered tabs.

Step 5

Now set something (not too heavy, like an eraser) on top of your die to hold it in place while it dries.

Movement Cube

Assembly Directions

1. Cut along the solid lines.
2. Fold along the dashed lines.
3. Tape or glue the cube together.

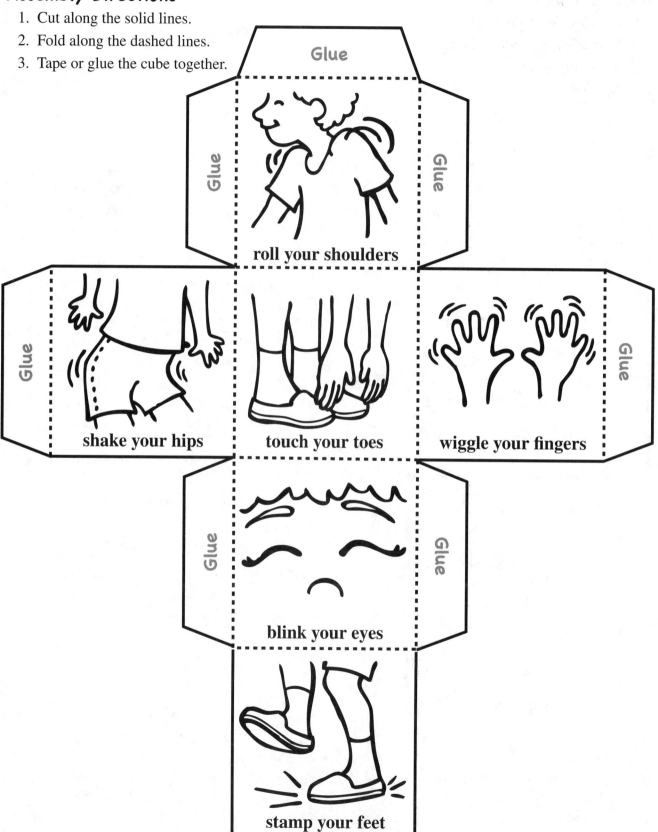

Blank Cube

Add specific pictures or text to the blank squares provided below to make your own cube.

Assembly Directions

1. Cut along the solid lines.
2. Fold along the dashed lines.
3. Tape or glue the cube together.

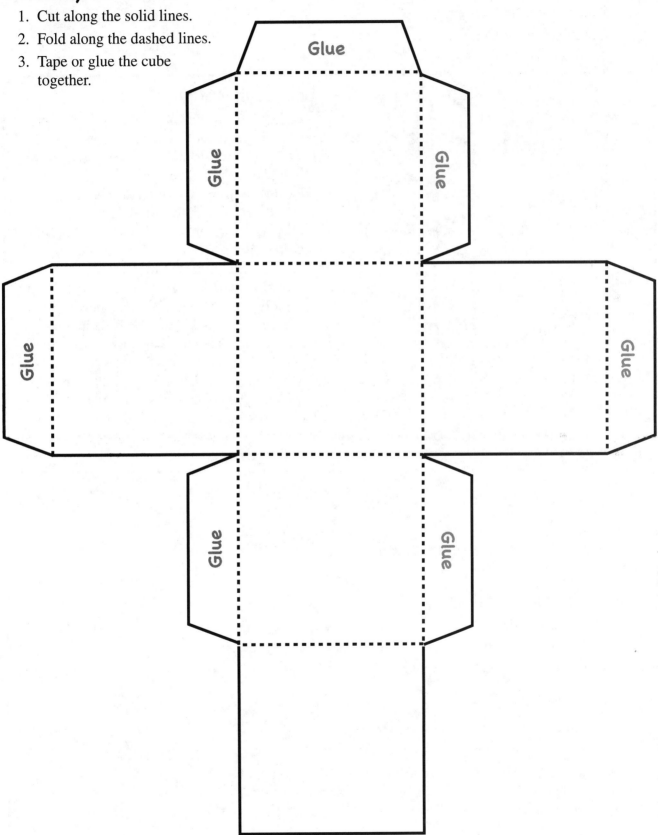

My Body *(cont.)*

◎ **Community Circle Activities** ◎

Identity

You will need a yardstick or broomstick for this activity.

Body Symmetry

Ask students to name parts of their bodies that come in pairs (hands, feet, legs, arms, eyes, ears, elbows, wrists, ankles, knees, lips, nostrils, etc.). Then ask them to name body parts that come in groups of five (fingers, toes, fingernails, knuckles, etc.). Finally, ask them to point out body parts of which we only have one (nose, mouth, belly button, etc.). Have a student volunteer stand in front of the class and place a yardstick or a broomstick in front of the student vertically, creating a midline (see illustration). Ask students to look at where the paired body parts are and where the single body parts are located. Lead students to discover that the single items are almost always in the center of our bodies, while the items in pairs are usually located one on each side of our midline.

Focus on the Face

Give students hand mirrors and ask them to look at their faces closely. Then ask them questions like the following:

You will need hand mirrors for this activity.

- How far can you stick out your tongue?
- Do you have freckles?
- What colors do you see in your eyes?
- Close your eyes for a moment and then open them quickly—what do your pupils do?
- Can you see your teeth when you smile?
- Can you wiggle your ears or your nose?

Keep asking questions as long as student interest is high.

My Body (cont.)

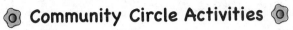

✹ Community Circle Activities ✹

That's the Spot!

Have students sit in pairs facing each other. Give each child a sheet of small stickers. Next, tell students to gently stick a sticker on a partner's nose. Then tell them to put a sticker on their partner's knee. Ask student volunteers to name other body parts and have students put stickers on them. At the end, be sure to take a picture of everyone covered with stickers!

You will need small stickers for this activity.

Super Senses

Place a cracker in front of each student, but tell them not to touch or eat it yet. Ask students if they can see the cracker. Then ask them what it looks like. Ask students, "What part of your bodies do you use to see it?" Next, ask students to touch the cracker. Then ask them what it feels like. Next ask them, "What part of your bodies do you use to feel it?" Ask students to smell the cracker. Then ask them what it smells like. What part of their bodies do they use to smell it? Ask students to break the cracker in half. Then ask them if they could hear it break. Next ask them, "What part of your bodies did you use to hear it?" Tell students they can now eat their crackers. Ask them what it tastes like. Then ask them, "What part of your bodies did you use to taste it?" Tell students that they used their five senses to find out about the cracker and that those five senses are how they find out all about the world around them. Try the same activity with other items in the classroom.

You will need crackers for this activity.

My Body *(cont.)*

◉ Independent Practice ◉

Life-sized Self Portraits

Have students lie down on large, white butcher paper and use a pencil to trace their outlines. Let them paint in their features and clothing to create life-sized self portraits. Remind students to be as accurate as possible with their hair color, eye color, etc. Let students practice naming body parts by placing the Body Parts Cards (pages 5–12) on the appropriate parts of their self-portraits.

You will need white butcher paper and paint for this activity.

Mix and Match

Take a full-body photo of each student and have the photos printed. Cut the photos, separating the heads from the bodies so you have one head and one body for each student. Place the heads and bodies at a center and let students practice matching them. They can also see what they would look like with someone else's body!

(**Note:** Do not do this activity with Polaroid™ photos. If they are cut apart, students could be exposed to chemicals in between the layers of the Polaroid™ prints.)

You will need a camera and the ability to print photos for this activity.

Healthy Habits

◎ **Community Circle Activities** ◎

Self-discipline & Responsibility

Healthy Habits Charades

Make one copy of each Healthy Habits mini poster (pages 20–27). You may want to color them and laminate them for durability.

Ask students, "What are some things that we can do to take care of our bodies?" After some discussion, show students the Healthy Habits mini posters and read each item to the class. Ask for a student volunteer to choose a Healthy Habits mini poster (without telling the class what was chosen) and pantomime the activity while the class tries to guess which healthy habit is being shown. Take turns acting out the habits until they have all been named.

Use the Healthy Habits mini posters for this activity!

Here are some ideas for exercises:

- Touch your toes and then reach for the sky
- Pretend to hula hoop
- Hop on one foot
- Run in place
- Do jumping jacks
- Arm circles

Exercise of the Day

Copy and paste together the calendar on pages 28–29, filling in the month and the numbers, and display it in the classroom. Each day ask a student to choose a simple exercise movement for the class to perform for one minute and record it on the calendar. At the end of the month, celebrate your exercise success with a healthy snack or a fun game.

Copy and display the calendar on pages 28–29.

Healthy Habits

I brush my teeth.

Healthy Habits

I comb my hair.

Healthy Habits

I take a bath or a shower.

Healthy Habits

I eat healthy foods.

Healthy Habits

I get enough sleep.

Healthy Habits

I exercise my body.

26

Healthy Habits

I wear my seatbelt.

See directions on page 19. Laminate this calendar for future use.

Exercise Builds Strong Bodies!

Sunday	Monday	Tuesday	Wednesday	Thursday	Friday	Saturday

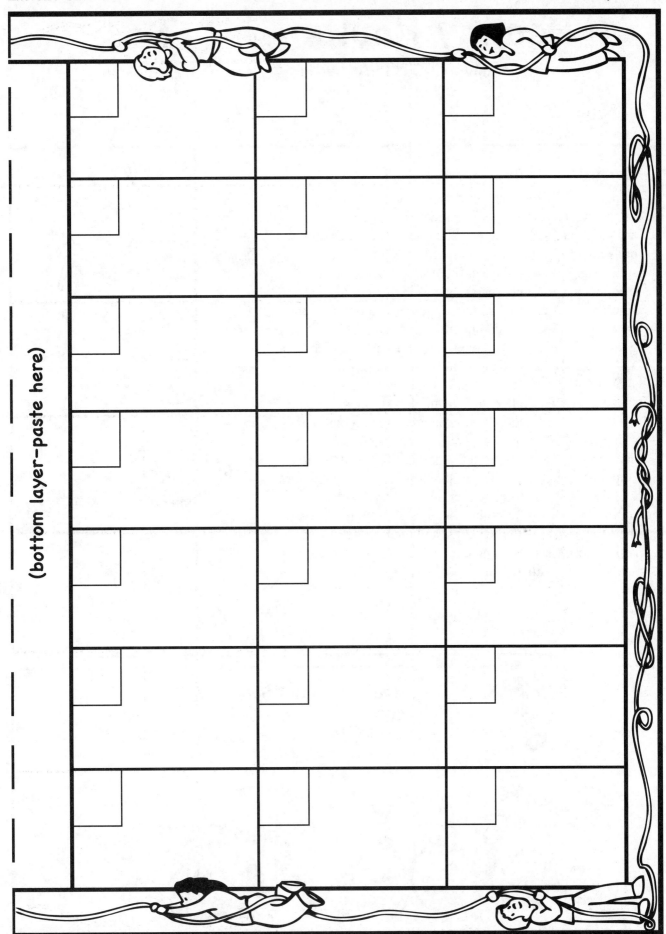

(bottom layer–paste here)

Healthy Habits (cont.)

⬡ **Community Circle Activities** ⬡

Self-discipline & Responsibility

Germs!

Explain to students that germs and viruses are living things that are too small to be seen with our eyes. Some are good for us and help our bodies do things like digest our food, but some germs and viruses can make us sick. Many times germs and viruses are passed from one person to another on our hands. Tell students that since germs are too small to see, you are going to do an experiment using glitter and pretend that the glitter is germs. Shake a small amount of glitter on your hand and shake several students' hands. Ask those students to show their hands to the class. Then have those students shake hands with other students until everyone has some "germs" on their hands. Tell students that they will be going to the sink and washing their hands, but they must do it properly to remove all the germs. Tell students to sing the "Happy Birthday" or the "Alphabet Song," while washing. Explain to them that this is to ensure that they scrub long enough. Remind students to wash in between their fingers, on both the palms, and the backs of their hands and wrists. Remind them also to rinse off all the soap and dry with a clean paper towel.

You will need glitter for this activity.

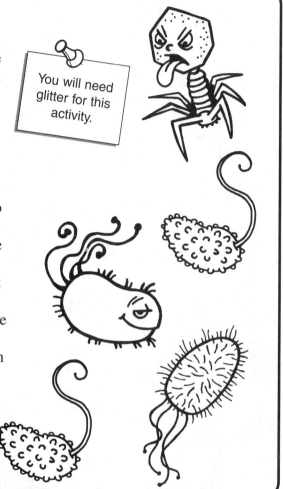

Healthy Habits Song

Copy and display the mini poster on page 31 and sing the "Healthy Habits Song" with your class. Be sure to have everyone act out the words!

Healthy Habits Song

(Sing to the tune of "Here We Go 'Round the Mulberry Bush" and act out the words.)

This is the way we wash our hands
Wash our hands, wash our hands.
This is the way we wash our hands
To keep our bodies healthy!

Other verses:
This is the way we brush our teeth . . .
This is the way we eat good food . . .
This is the way we exercise . . .
This is the way we go to sleep . . .

Healthy Habits (cont.)

⬡ **Small Group Activities** ⬡

Self-discipline & Responsibility

Wash Your Hands!

Give each student a piece of construction paper in a color similar to his or her skin tone (or use white paper and have students color it with crayons). Then have students trace one of their hands. Again using the crayons, students can decorate the hands with sleeves, bracelets, rings, fingernails, etc. Have students cut out the hands or cut the hands out for them if they are not developmentally ready to do it themselves. Ask students to tell you when they should wash their hands and write each answer on one of the cut-out hands. Display the hands near your classroom sink as a reminder to wash!

Here are some examples!

- Wash your hands after using the bathroom.

- Wash your hands before eating.

- Wash your hands after sneezing or coughing.

- Wash your hands after playing outdoors.

- Wash your hands after touching pets.

- Wash your hands when putting on a bandage.

You will need paper, pencils, crayons, and scissors for this activity.

You will need safety equipment such as helmets and knee pads for this activity.

Staying Safe on the Move

Borrow some safety equipment for bicycling, skating/skateboarding, and riding in a car. Bring the equipment in to show the class. Let students try on items like a helmet, knee pads, elbow pads, and a car seat. Describe how each item can keep them safe.

Healthy Habits *(cont.)*

Independent Practice

Brush and Floss

Show students an upside-down egg carton and ask them to pretend that the cells of the egg carton are big teeth. Using a toothbrush and dental floss, demonstrate how to brush thoroughly and floss in between the "teeth." Let students practice brushing and flossing the "big teeth." If children are old enough to be trusted not to put things in their mouths you can use shaving cream as "toothpaste."

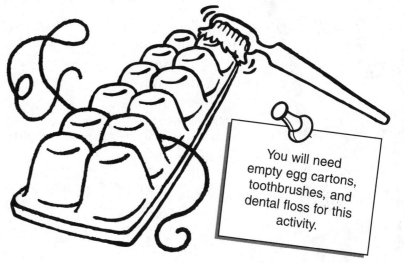

You will need empty egg cartons, toothbrushes, and dental floss for this activity.

Cover Up that Sneeze!

You will need the pattern (on page 34), scissors, crayons, glue, and tissues for this activity.

Show students how to use a tissue to cover their noses and mouths when they sneeze. If they do not have a tissue, they should sneeze into their shoulder or elbow. Give each student a copy of page 34. Ask students to color the face the color of their skin and draw their eyes, nose, mouth, and hair with crayons. Next, have students trace their hand onto a piece of paper and cut it out. Next, color it the color of their hand. Show students how to glue a tissue to the inside of the hand and then glue the hand onto the face to cover up the sneeze.

Relationships Environment

I Take Care of my Body Minibook

You will need crayons or markers for this activity.

Copy and assemble the I Take Care of my Body minibook on pages 35–38 for each student. Have students color each page with crayons or markers.

Cover Up That Sneeze!

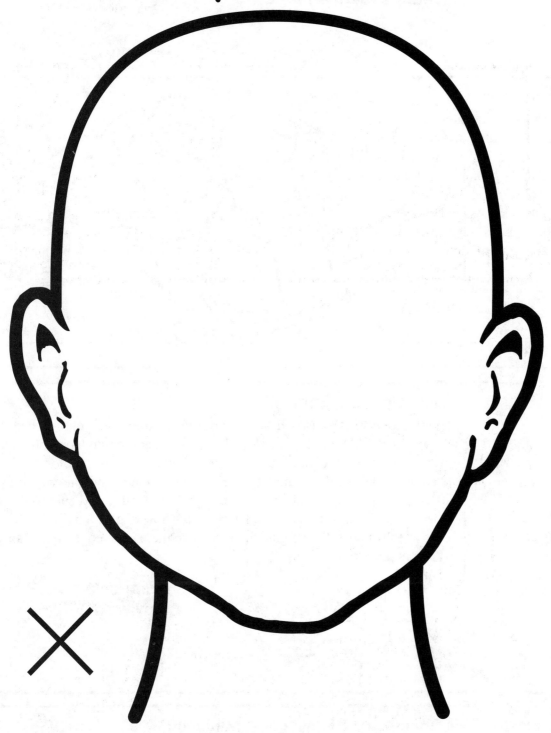

Directions: Color the face to look like you. Trace your hand, cut it out, and glue the base (wrist) of it to the **X**. Glue a tissue to the inside of the hand to cover your mouth and nose. This is how to keep your germs to yourself!

I Take Care of my Body

By: _____

I brush my teeth.

1

I comb my hair. **2**

I take a bath or a shower. **3**

I wash my hands.

I eat healthy foods. **5**

I get enough sleep. 6

I exercise my body. 7

I Am Unique

⬡ **Community Circle Activities** ⬡

**Relationships
Identity**

Who Is "It"?

Ask the class to stand. Select a student to be "it," but don't tell the class whom you have chosen. Select an attribute of that student, such as black hair, and tell the class, "This person has black hair." Ask for all students who do not have black hair to sit down. Call out something else about the student, such as, "This person loves to play on the swings at recess," and ask the remaining students who do not play on the swings to sit down. Continue until "it" is the only student left standing. Review the attributes that make the student unique; "Shelby is the only student in our class who has black hair, plays on the swings at recess, speaks Japanese, and eats peanut butter for lunch every day." You can do a couple of rounds of this activity each day until every student has had a turn. You may want to write down the results on the I Am Unique parent letter (page 40) to send home with students as a reminder of how special they are! This could take several days.

Name Cheers

Write a student's name on the board in large letters. Have students do a cheer for that student using each letter of the name; "Give me a D!" "D!" "Give me an A!" "A!" "Give me an N!" "N!" "What does that spell?" "Dan!" You'll be practicing letter recognition while celebrating each individual student.

You will need a baby names book for this activity.

What's in a Name?

Send home a copy of the letter on page 41 asking parents to write about the origin of their child's name. After students have returned their name origins, read each one aloud (without saying the name) and let the class guess whose name you are describing. If some students do not return the form, you can look up the meanings of their names in a baby names book.

**Identity
Culture**

Dear Families,

As part of our unit focusing on how each student is special, we played a game in class today that shows how each student is unique. The things that make your child different from everyone else in our class are listed below. Celebrate your child's unique qualities!

_____is the only student in our class who

_____

_____

_____

_____

_____

_____

_____

Sincerely,

_____

Dear Parents,

As part of our "I Am Unique" unit, we would like to explore the origins of your children's names. In the space below, please write a brief description of how you chose your child's name, and we will share it with the class.

Child's Name:_____

Below are some questions to help get started:

- How long did it take to decide on the name?

- Did you wait until your child was born or choose a name earlier?

- Did you choose a name and then change your mind after your child was born?

- Is your child named after a family member?

- Was your child named after someone you admire?

- Is the name indicative of your family's heritage?

- Does the name have a meaning?

- Did you use a baby name book?

- Who helped choose the name?

If needed, use the back of this page for other stories about how this name was chosen.

_____

_____

_____

_____

_____

_____

Thank you,

_____

I Am Unique

⚙ **Independent Practice** ⚙

Unique Voices

Individually and away from the other students, record each student's voice saying a poem, singing a song, or reading aloud. Play back the recordings for the class and let students guess who each one is.

You will need an audio recorder for this activity.

You will need a washable stamp pad for this activity.

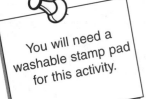

Fun with Fingerprints

Explain to students that no two people have the same fingerprints. Show students how to press and roll their fingers on a washable stamp pad and then press their fingers on paper to make fingerprints. Provide magnifying glasses and let students observe and describe the lines, swirls, and whorls, then compare their fingerprints to other students' fingerprints. You may want to provide examples for students of each type of the prints mentioned.

You will need pencils and crayons or markers for this activity.

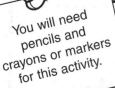

All About Me Books

Copy, cut apart, and assemble the A Book About _____ (fill in the student's name) minibook on pages 43–48 for each student. Students can illustrate each page and then write or dictate to fill in the blanks. Encourage students to share their completed books with the class. Students could work on the minibook pages over an extended period of time.

A Book About_____.

My name is

_____
first name

_____
middle name

_____.
last name

1

I am ⬭ years old.

2

My birthday is_____.

3

Draw a picture of your home.

My street address is

_____ .

My phone number is

_____ _____

_____ _____

My favorite food is _____. **6**

I like the color _____.

At home I like to _____. **8**

At school I like to _____. **9**

I am good at_____.

I want to learn to_____.

I Am Unique *(cont.)*
◉ Community Circle Activities ◉

What's My Number?

Create a card for each student with his or her name and phone number. At a center, set out a few non-working telephones along with the phone number cards and let students practice dialing their home numbers.

You will need non-working telephones for this activity. They are often available at garage sales or thrift stores. Remove any batteries before giving the telephones to students.

You will need paper, a stapler, and crayons or markers for this activity.

Name Book

Create a blank book for each student by folding several sheets of blank drawing paper in half and stapling at the fold. Write each student's name clearly on the front of a book. On each page, write a letter of the student's name. Have students illustrate something that starts with each letter of their names.

Feelings

◉ Community Circle Activities ◉

Focus on Feelings

Tell students that you are going to talk about feelings. Explain that most people don't feel happy all the time—they may have many different feelings in a day. Sometimes people have two different feelings at the same time! Ask students to name some feelings that they know (*happy, sad, angry*) and tell about a time when they felt that way. Show students the Feelings Cube (page 51) and tell them that they are going to play a feelings game. Roll the cube like a die and show students the face that comes up on top. Have them make the face shown. Ask them to name the feeling (there may be more than one answer) and talk about when they might feel that way.

Body Language

In the Feelings Cube game students focused on showing feelings through their faces. Tell them that this time they will show feelings with their bodies. Sing "If You're Happy and You Know It" (see page 52 for some different verse ideas) and have students do the movements. After each verse, discuss the feelings students acted out and think of other ways to express them.

Cut out and assemble the Feelings Cube (on page 51).

Mirror Game

Pair students up and ask one student in each pair to show a feeling. The second student should mirror or copy the first student, then tell what they think the feeling is.

Sing a Song of Feelings

Copy the mini poster on page 52 and sing "If You're Happy and You Know It," focusing on feelings.

Feelings Cube

Assembly Directions

1. Cut along the solid lines.
2. Fold along the dashed lines.
3. Tape or glue the cube together.

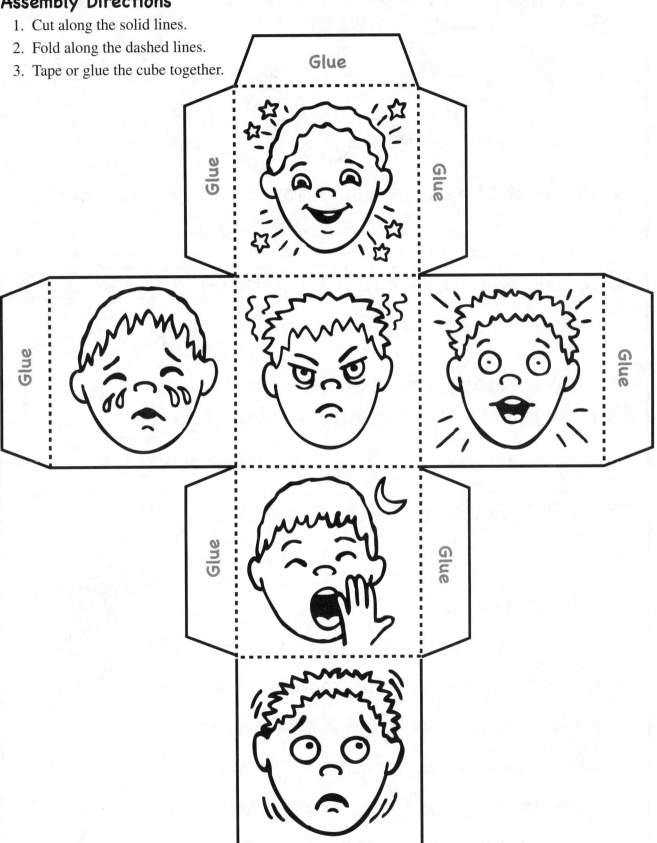

If You're Happy And You Know It

(Traditional)

If you're happy and you know it, clap your hands.

(clap, clap)

If you're happy and you know it, clap your hands.

(clap, clap)

If you're happy and you know it,
then your face will really show it.

(Make a happy face.)

If you're happy and you know it, clap your hands.

(clap, clap)

Additional Verses

If you're angry and you know it, *stomp your feet.*

If you're frightened and you know it, *cover your eyes.*

If you're tired and you know it, *give a yawn.*

If you're silly and you know it, *tickle your tummy.*

If you're sad and you know it, *hang your head.*

If you're excited and you know it, *jump around.*

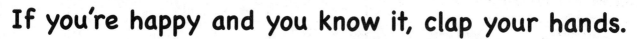

Feelings *(cont.)*
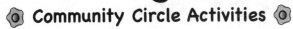
◎ Community Circle Activities ◎

Identity Relationships

Mirror Feelings
Cut out magazine pictures of children expressing different feelings or take photographs of your students and have them printed. Set the photos out at a center with a mirror and let students practice copying the expressions. You can also create word cards for the different feelings and have students match the word cards to the pictures.

You will need a mirror and magazines, or a camera and the ability to print photos for this activity.

Feelings Minibook
Copy and assemble the Feelings minibook on pages 54–56 for each student. Have students write or dictate to fill in the blanks on each page and then illustrate.

Feelings Faces
Copy the two Feelings Faces pages (pages 57–58) for each student. Give each student a copy of each Feelings Faces page, scissors, and a glue stick. Encourage students to choose a pair of eyes and a mouth, color and cut them out, and glue them onto the blank face. Encourage students to tell you about the feelings that they have created.

You will need scissors, crayons, and glue sticks for this activity.

When I Am Angry

Self-discipline & Respect

Talk with students about times that they have felt angry or frustrated. What happened that made them feel that way? What did they do about it? Did the effort make them feel better? Display a copy of the When I Am Angry mini poster (page 59) and discuss some of the things students can do to make themselves feel better when they are angry.

Feelings

I feel happy when_____.

I feel sad when_____.

I feel angry when_____. **2**

I feel shy when_____. **3**

I feel afraid when_____.

I feel excited when_____. 5

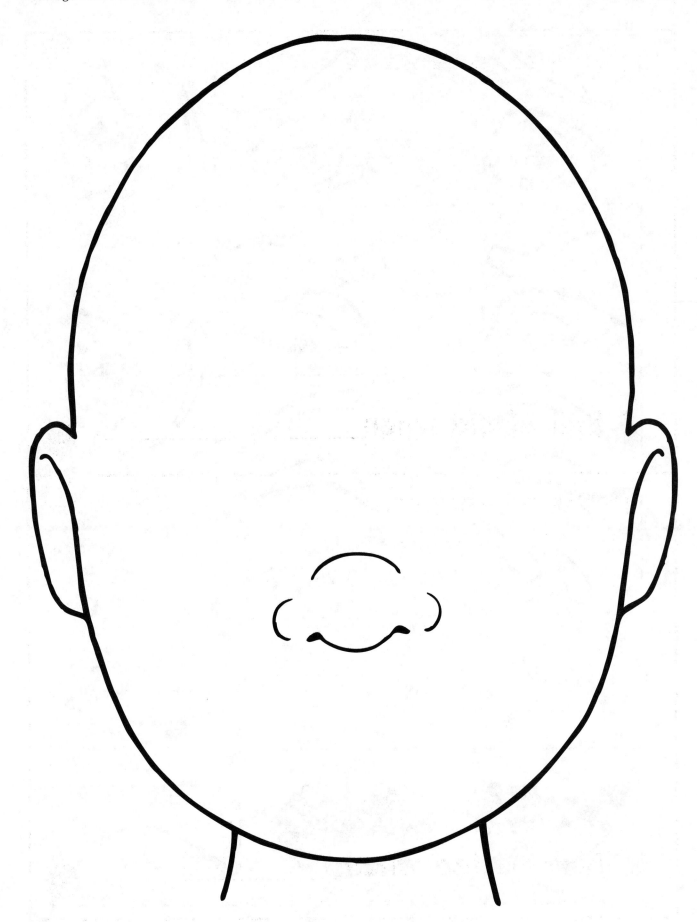

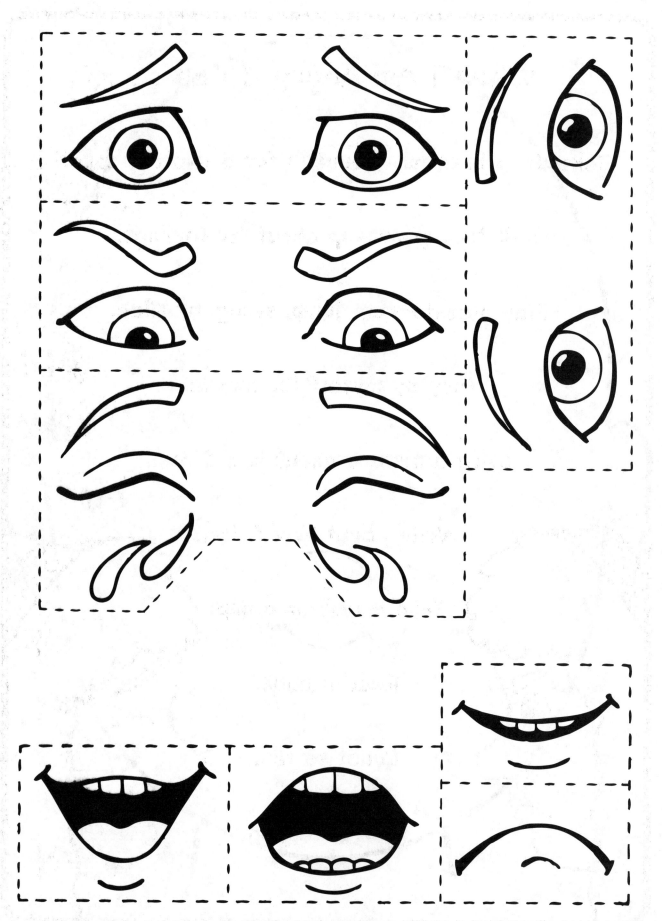

When I Am Angry, I Can . . .

Take deep breaths. Count in for 5 and out for 5!

Talk to a grown-up about my feelings.

Play outside—run, jump, swing, or slide.

Play by myself for awhile.

Draw a picture about how I feel.

Write about how I feel.

Take a rest or a nap.

Read a book.

Count to ten.

Then try again.

Independence

◉ Community Circle Activities ◉

Identity

Growing Up

Have students bring in photos of themselves as babies. Have each student stand in front of the class and show his or her baby photo. Students can point out the physical differences and changes in each child ("You have more hair now." "You have all your teeth."). While holding the photo have the student tell some things that he or she could not do as a baby that he or she can do now—record the answers on a piece of chart paper.

Students will need to bring in their baby photos for this activity.

I Can Do It! Minibook

Copy and assemble the I Can Do It! minibook on page 61 for each student. You may make as many pages as you like for each book. Display the chart paper from the Growing Up group lesson. Students can copy or dictate to fill in the blanks on the pages of their books and illustrate.

Perseverance

I Can Do It!

When I was a baby I couldn't_____,

but now I can do it all by myself!

When I was a baby I couldn't_____,

but now I can do it all by myself!

Independence *(cont.)*

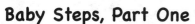 Community Circle Activities

Baby Steps, Part One

Make a copy of the Baby Steps Cutouts (page 63) for each group and cut out the pieces.

Ask students to think about what happened the first time they tried something new, like riding a bike. Were they able to do it right away? What did they do if they failed the first time? Tell students that if something is difficult to do all at once, they can take "baby steps" to achieve their goal, which means doing a little bit at a time. Ask students to think of something that they haven't done at school that they would like to try (going across the monkey bars without letting go or writing their own name.)

Choose one activity and have the group brainstorm "baby steps" that they could take to achieve the goal. For example, if the goal is to write their names, baby steps might be to write one letter, then add the other letters one at a time, or to practice tracing the letters in their names. If the goal is to make it across the monkey bars, baby steps might be to swing from the first rung to the second, then add the third, etc. As the group chooses the baby steps, write each on a footprint and place it in a pocket chart or on a bulletin board, lining the baby steps up like footprints. Write the final goal on the You Did It! card and place it at the end.

You will need to make copies of page 63 for students.

Baby Steps, Part Two

Copy the Baby Steps Worksheet on page 64, making one for every three students and cut apart the three strips. Help each student choose a goal and create baby steps toward reaching that goal. Record the goal and planned steps on the Baby Steps Worksheet (page 64). Display the worksheets in the classroom. As students take their baby steps, let them color in the appropriate footprints on their worksheets. Celebrate when they reach their goals!

Perseverance

You Did It!

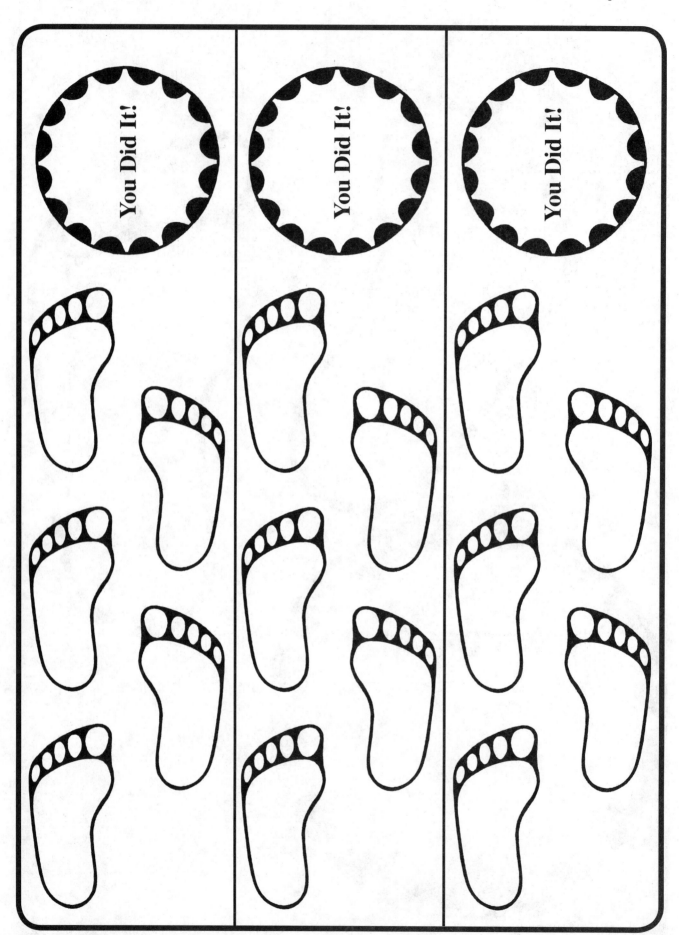

Independence *(cont.)*

⬡ **Community Circle Activities** ⬡

Environment

I Can Dress Myself

Gather items of clothing for different types of weather. (jacket, scarf, mittens, hat, long pants, shorts, short-sleeved shirt, dress, turtleneck, swimsuit, sun hat, etc.)

Tell students that one thing they can learn to do by themselves is to get dressed in the morning. Name a type of weather (sunny, rainy, snowy) and have a student pick out and put on appropriate clothing (over his or her own clothing), then "model" for the group. Discuss how the clothing helps us in each type of weather (When it is cold, mittens keep our hands warm.) What would happen if students wore each type of clothing in the wrong weather? (If you wore a hat, jacket, and mittens on a hot day, you would be too hot!)

You will need items of clothing for different types of weather.

Weather Matching

Copy the Weather Matching Pictures (pages 66–68) and cut them out. If possible, color them and laminate them for durability.

Set the Weather Matching Picture Cards (pages 69–71) out at a center and let students practice matching each article of clothing to the appropriate weather.

You will need old shoes and clothing for this activity.

Buttons and Bows

At a center, set out several pairs of old shoes with laces, some jackets with zippers, and shirts with buttons so students can practice tying, zipping, and buttoning.

Self-discipline

Rainy Day

Sunny Day

Snowy Day

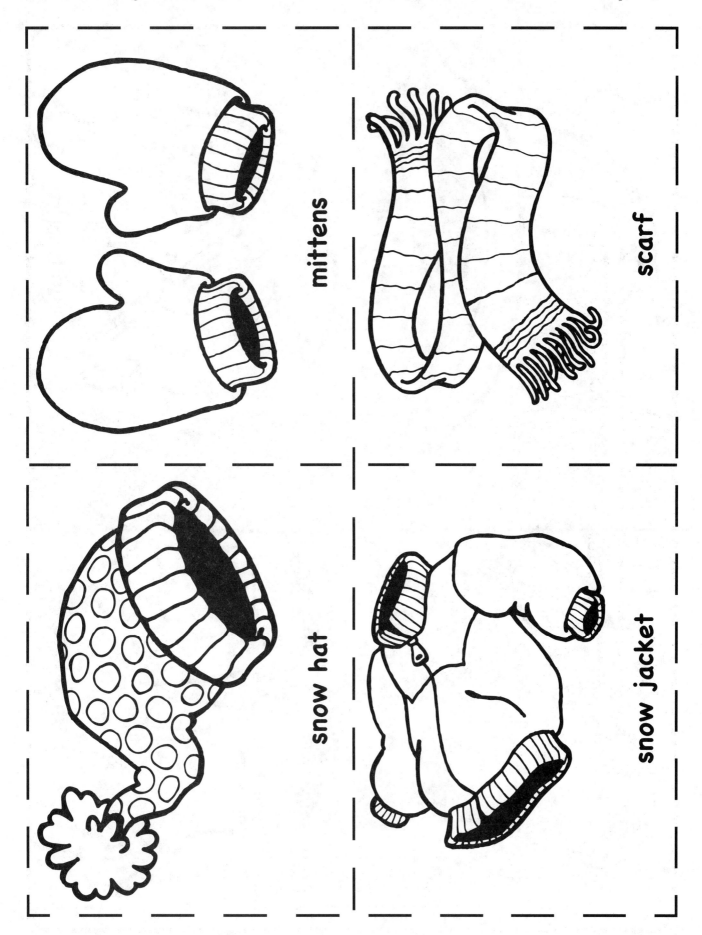

mittens

scarf

snow hat

snow jacket

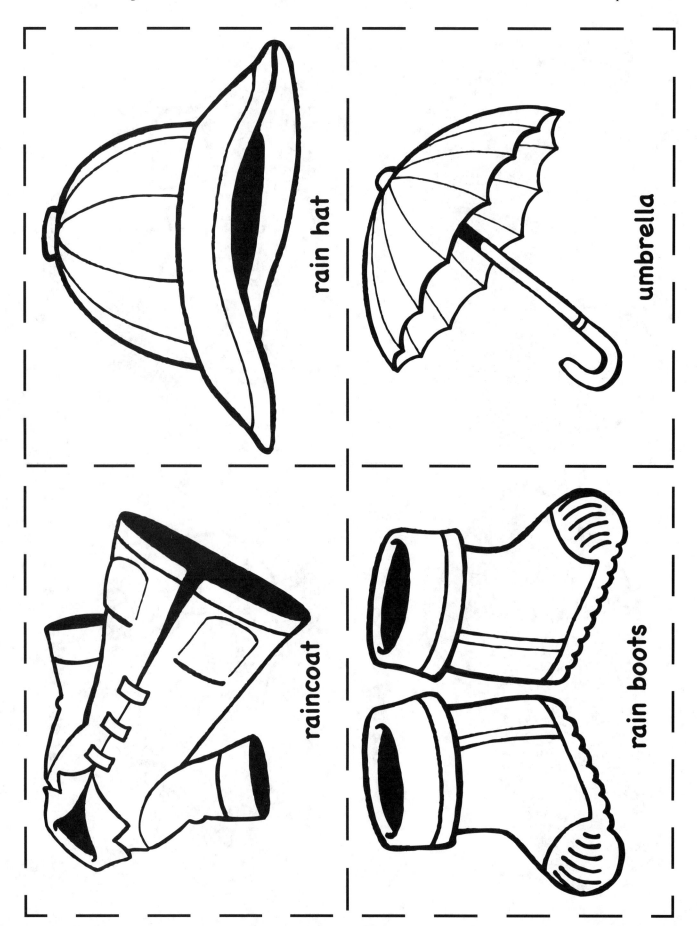

rain hat

umbrella

raincoat

rain boots

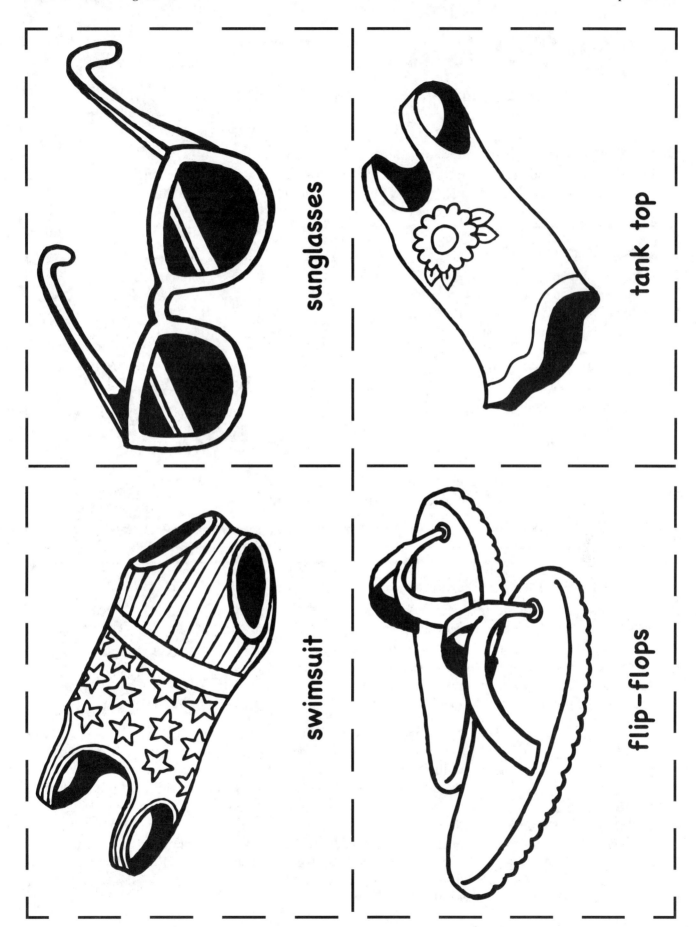

sunglasses

tank top

swimsuit

flip-flops

What is a Family?

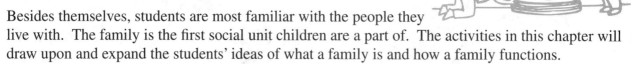

@ **Community Circle Activities** @

Culture
Relationships

Besides themselves, students are most familiar with the people they live with. The family is the first social unit children are a part of. The activities in this chapter will draw upon and expand the students' ideas of what a family is and how a family functions.

What Is a Family?

Talk with students about what "family" means. Some families consist of a mother, father, and children, but there are many other types of families. Some students may have two homes because of a divorce and some may live with grandparents or other relatives. Some may live with caregivers who are not blood relations. Do all members of a family have to live in the same home together? Discuss what makes each of these a "family" (loving one another, taking care of each other, doing things together, etc.). Record students' ideas about what makes a family on chart paper, title it "Family Is…," and display it in the classroom.

You will need chart paper and markers for this activity.

Getting to Know our Families

Tell students that over the next few days they will be getting to know each other's families. Start by showing photos of your own family and pets. Tell students about your family members as you show the photos. Invite students to ask questions and be as honest as you can in your answers. When you are finished, display your photos on a bulletin board and, if you like, add captions for your photos.

Kindness & Respect

Send a copy of the Getting to Know Our Families Letter on page 73 home with each student. This letter asks parents to send in photos of their families. It will be easier for students to sit and listen if there are no more than three students sharing their photos each day, so schedule student sharing days accordingly. As students bring in their photos, ask them to show and describe each photo and answer questions from the class. Display students' photos on a bulletin board along with your own so that students can look at them throughout the day. Make sure that they are displayed at student eye-level.

Date:_____

Dear Families,

As part of our study of families, we ask that your child bring
a few family photos to share with the class. The photos should
show as many different family members as possible. We will be
as careful as possible with all photos, but you may want to have
copies made of any photos that cannot be replaced and send the
copies to school instead of the originals.

Your child's photo sharing day will be_____

   Thank you,

_____

Date:_____

Dear Families,

As part of our study of families, we ask that your child bring
a few family photos to share with the class. The photos should
show as many different family members as possible. We will be
as careful as possible with all photos, but you may want to have
copies made of any photos that cannot be replaced and send the
copies to school instead of the originals.

Your child's photo sharing day will be_____

   Thank you,

_____

What is a Family? *(cont.)*

Culture Relationships

Community Circle Activities

Family Graph of the Day

Use these graph questions to create a "Family Graph of the Day" during your study of families.

- How many people live in your home with you?

- How many brothers and sisters (siblings) do you have?

- How many aunts and uncles do you have?

- How many cousins do you have?

- How many of your family members are boys?

- How many of your family members are girls?

- What pets does your family have? How many pets do you have?

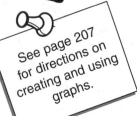

See page 207 for directions on creating and using graphs.

Family "Who Am I?"

Play Family "Who Am I?" with your students. Describe a family member by his or her relationship to students (see examples below) and ask students to name the family member.

- I am your (mother or father)'s mother. *Grandmother*

- I am your (mother or father)'s father. *Grandfather*

- I am your (mother or father)'s sister. *Aunt*

- I am your (mother or father)'s brother. *Uncle*

- I am your (aunt or uncle)'s child. *Cousin*

- I am a girl and your parents are the same as mine. *Sister*

- I am a boy and your parents are the same as mine. *Brother*

What is a Family? *(cont.)*

◉ Community Circle Activities ◉

Family Names, Part One

We often use different terms to refer to
members of our family. On chart paper, create
columns with these headings: mother, father,
sister, brother, grandmother, grandfather. You
could also add aunt, uncle, cousin, or any other
appropriate family member. Be aware that
some of your students may have non-traditional
family structures and adjust accordingly.
As you read each word aloud, ask students
to tell you what they call that relative and
record it on the chart. For example, "Mother"
might be Mom, Mommy, Madre, or Mama.
"Grandfather" could be Papa, Pere, Abuelo,
Papi, or Grandpa. Save this chart for Family
Names, Part Two.

You will need
chart paper and
markers for this
activity.

Family Names, Part Two

Review with students the chart you created in Family Names,
Part One. Ask students to think about all the names that
they are called. Call out a role (daughter, son, sister, brother,
granddaughter, grandson, niece, nephew, cousin, etc.) and ask
students to stand up if that role describes them. Each of these
roles might have a special name, so ask students to tell the
group what they are called in their family. Encourage students
to use complete sentences ("My grandmother calls me
Mija," or "My brother calls me Sissy."). Give each
student a copy of My Special Names Worksheet on
page 79 and help him or her write or dictate all
the special names that are theirs.

What is a Family? *(cont.)*

⊚ Independent Practice ⊚

Culture Relationships

Family Paper Dolls

Copy the Family Paper Dolls (pages 77–78) on heavy paper. If students are not developmentally ready to cut out the paper dolls, precut them. Ask students to select dolls to represent members of their families and color them. Students can add yarn hair, fabric clothing, or other materials to complete their paper dolls. When the dolls are finished, mount each family on a large piece of construction paper, aligning them so they are "holding hands." Ask students to write or dictate the name of each family member.

You will need craft or art materials for this activity.

Family Sorting

Gather some old magazines and cut out pictures of household items, some that adults would use, some that students would use, and some that are for a baby (baby clothes/children's clothes/adult clothes, baby bottle/child's spoon/steak knife, etc.). Title each of three large pieces of construction paper, "Things for Grown–Ups," "Things for Babies," and "Things for Me." Have students sort the pictures onto the three papers and then glue them down to create collages. Display the collages in the classroom.

Responsibility

Housekeeping Corner

Set up a Housekeeping Corner for free play. Include dress-up clothes so students can pretend to be different members of a family, and some baby dolls with clothing and accessories so students can practice caregiving. Add household items such as empty food containers and dishes and tools for housework.

My _____ calls me _____ .

My _____ calls me _____ .

Family Culture

◉ **Community Circle Activities** ◉

Culture Relationships

Family Fun, Part One

Ask students to name some of the things they enjoy doing with their families. Examples might include preparing and eating meals together, reading together, going for a walk, playing a game, or going to the movies. Record each response on chart paper and then ask everyone whose family also likes to do that activity to stand up. Have students help you count the number of students standing and write that number next to the activity. When you have about ten activities listed, discuss the findings. Were there some activities that were very popular? Which ones? Were there any activities that only a few families liked to do? Are there some activities that you would like to try with your family? Save the list for Family Fun, Part Two.

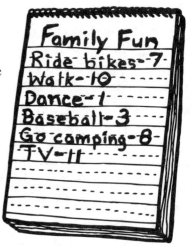

You will need chart paper for this activity.

Family Fun, Part Two

Review with students the list of activities from Family Activities, Part One. Give students blank paper and ask them to illustrate one activity that their family does together. (It does not have to be on the list.) Have students write or dictate a sentence on their pages. Put all the pages together, add a cover, and make a class book titled, "Family Fun."

Cooperation

Family Culture *(cont.)*

🌸 Community Circle Activities 🌸

Culture
Relationships

Sharing Family Traditions

Explain to the class that a tradition is something that a group of people do in the same way over and over for many years. Tell the class about some traditions in your family, such as how you celebrate birthdays or holidays or other everyday traditions. Send home a copy of the letter on page 82, asking students' families to talk about their traditions and share a related article from one of them. When children return with their objects representing family traditions, ask them to share with the class.

Traditional celebrations can include ceremonies, songs, decorations, special foods, or special clothing. Everyday traditions can be anything from a special way of reading bedtime stories to the seating arrangements at the family dinner table.

Favorite Family Traditions

Ask students to choose their favorite family tradition and paint a picture of it. When the paintings are dry, have students write or dictate a sentence about their pictures. Gather all of the paintings into a big book titled "Our Favorite Family Traditions."

We break a piñata at every holiday.

We celebrate everyone's birthday.

We go to watch the big fireworks every 4th of July.

Respect

Date:_____

Dear Families,

As part of our study of families, we will be discussing family traditions. Using the discussion guide below, please take time over the next few days to talk with your child about your family's traditions and celebrations.

On _____, please have your child bring one object (or a picture of an object) that represents a family tradition to share with the class. We hope this will be a fun and rewarding experience for your whole family.

Sincerely,

_____

☐ **Day One:** What small, everyday traditions does your family keep? (Examples: reading a bedtime story under the covers, special seating arrangements at the dinner table, family game or movie night, baking cookies together, hugging everyone in the family before going to bed). Choose one example and discuss how that tradition came to be in your family.

☐ **Day Two:** What holidays does your family celebrate? Which holiday is your child's favorite? Discuss the traditions and customs associated with that holiday, such as special food, clothing, music, ceremonies, or decorations.

☐ **Day Three:** What other special days does your family celebrate? (Examples: birthdays, weddings, anniversaries, adoption days, loss of a baby tooth, the first day of a new school year). Choose one example and discuss how your family celebrates.

☐ **Day Four:** As a family, choose one object that represents one of your family traditions, large or small, and have your child bring it (or a photo of it) to school. Your child will be asked to share this object with the class and tell about your family tradition.

Family Culture *(cont.)*

⚙ Community Circle Activities ⚙

Culture
Relationships
Geography

Family Geography

Send a copy of the letter on page 84 home with each student. This letter asks parents to help students identify their birthplaces and their parents' birthplaces. When students return the letters to school, gather them in small groups and help them mark their family origins on a large map with sticky notes, writing the pertinent information on each—"Jung's father was born in Korea," or "Shelby was born in Arizona." Depending on students' backgrounds, you may need a U.S. or world map. Display the map in the classroom.

Respect

Family Geography, Alternate Version

On Back-to-School or Parent night, display a world map in the classroom and ask parents and caregivers to mark their birthplaces and their children's birthplaces on the map. When children return to school, show them the map and talk about where their families are from.

You will need a large U.S. or world map for this activity.

Ciaran

Shelby

Liam

Shelley

Becky

Sarah

Date:_____

Dear Parents,

As part of our study of families, we are creating a large map showing the family origins of our students. Please help your child fill in the following sentences and send this letter back to class. Feel free to skip any items that do not apply to your family or add any sentences you would like.

                                        Thank you,

                        _____

I was born in_____.

My mother was born in_____.

My father was born in_____.

My _____ was born in _____.

My _____ was born in _____.

Many Kinds of Homes

◎ Community Circle Activities ◎

Home Sorting

Ask each student to describe his or her home. Discuss the different rooms in students' homes and how they are used. Set out three large boxes labeled "Bathroom," "Bedroom," and "Kitchen." Show students a variety of objects that they might find in one of these three rooms and have a student volunteer place each object in the correct box. Keep in mind that some items might have more than one proper placement. For example, a hairbrush could go in the bathroom or the bedroom. Encourage students to explain their choices.

For this activity you will need three large boxes and assorted household items.

Some Items for Sorting:

- pot or pan
- silverware
- spatula
- roll of toilet paper
- hand soap
- hairbrush
- shampoo
- stuffed animal
- articles of clothing

Home Sorting Worksheet

Copy the Home Sorting Worksheet (page 86) for each child. Ask students to cut out the items on the dotted lines and then glue or paste the items in the appropriate rooms.

Many Kinds of Homes *(cont.)*

 Community Circle Activities

Many Different Homes

Ask students, "Why do people need homes?" (For shelter from the weather, to keep them safe, to store their belongings). Show students the mini posters of different homes (pages 88–93). Discuss how each home is different from students' homes and how they are similar. Talk about how each home is specially made for the place where it is built. Talk about what might happen if someone tried to live in an igloo in the desert or a grass hut on the ocean!

Homes Matching

Cut out and laminate the Homes Matching cards on pages 94–95 (the cards match the items discussed in Many Different Homes). Help students match each home to its environment, encouraging language development by asking students to state where each home belongs and why; "The houseboat belongs in the water because it can float," or "The apartment goes in the city so lots of people can live there."

Houseboat

It floats on the water. It is made to be in the ocean or on a river or lake.

Apartment

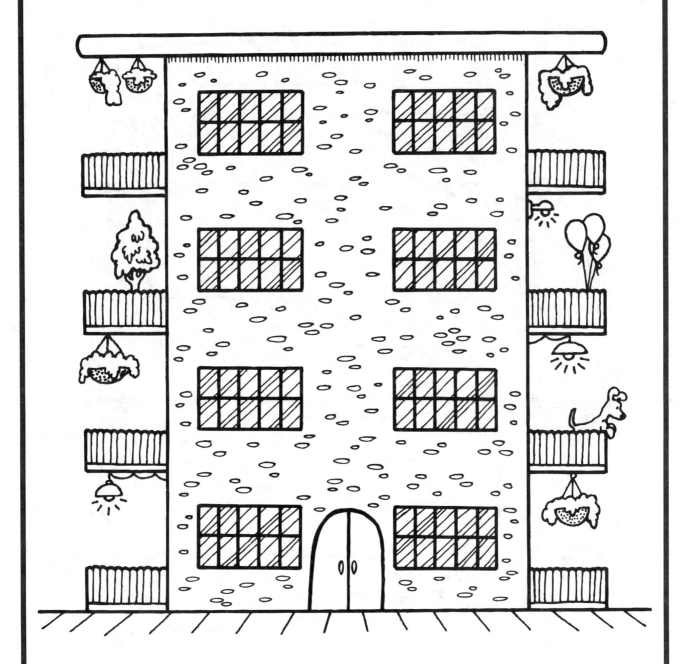

Many people can live on a smaller piece of land. It is made to be in the city.

Camper or RV

It can be moved to many different places.

Stilt Home

It is raised up so floods or tides can go underneath. It is made to be near the ocean or a river that floods.

Igloo

It is built from ice. It is generally used for shelter while hunting, not as a home all of the time. It is made to be used where there is always ice and snow.

Grass or Thatched Hut

It is made from grass that grows nearby. It stays cool in the heat. It is made to be used in a hot climate.

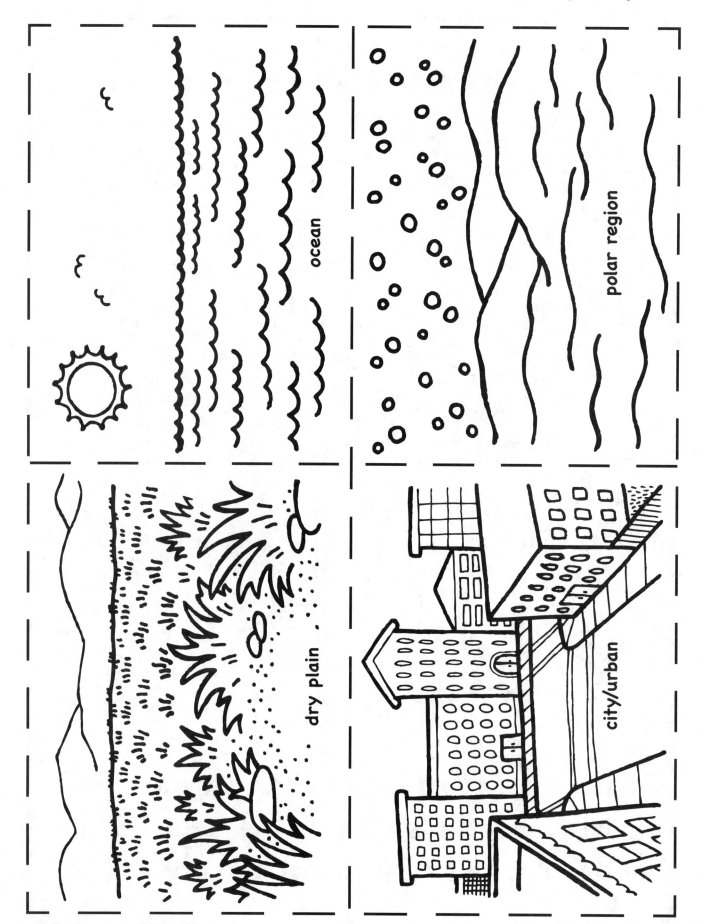

ocean

polar region

dry plain

city/urban

houseboat

igloo

grass hut

apartment

Many Kinds of Homes *(cont.)*

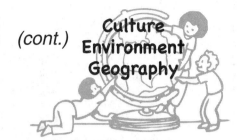

Culture
Environment
Geography

🔵 **Community Circle Activities** 🔵

Create a Home

Supply students with various materials (boxes, cardboard tubes, construction paper, tin foil, clean food containers, glue, glitter, etc.) and ask them to build an unusual home for their family. Tell them to think about where their home will be located and build it to fit the environment. For example, if they want to build a home that will be under the ocean, it needs to keep air in and water out. A flying house needs a way to stay up in the air. Encourage language development by asking students to dictate names and descriptions of the homes they built. Display the homes and descriptions in the classroom.

You will need craft and recycled materials for this project.

Our House

Turn a large appliance box (big enough for several children to fit inside) upside down and cut a door and some windows in the sides. Set out paint or markers for students to decorate the house and let them play inside.

You will need a large cardboard box and paints or markers for this activity.

Family as Community

Community Circle Activities

Culture
Relationships
Civics

Rules at Home

Ask students to think about some rules they have in their homes. You may want to give them some examples, such as "Stay away from the stove," or "Pick your toys up off of the floor." Discuss with students the reason behind each rule; "We shouldn't touch the stove because we could get burned," and "We should pick up our toys so no one will trip and get hurt."

Helping at Home

Talk with the class about how each of their family members helps at home. Ask students to think about what might happen if family members stopped helping. What would happen if no one made dinner? What would happen if no one fed the dog? What would happen if no one cleaned the house? As a class, write a story entitled, "The Day That Nobody Helped."

Nobody fed Hector.

We Can Help!

Encourage students to think about their own roles in their families. How do they help? Ask student volunteers to pantomime chores they do at home and have students try to guess which chore is being shown. As each chore is named, ask students to raise their hands or stand up if they do that chore at home.

Washing the car!

Responsibility & Citizenship

Family as Community *(cont.)*

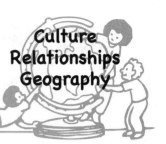

**Culture
Relationships
Geography**

Community Circle Activities

Helping Song

Sing the "Helping Song," using student suggestions to create new verses. Be sure to have students act out each verse!

(Sung to the tune of "Here We Go 'Round the Mulberry Bush")

**This is the way I set the table,
set the table, set the table**

This is the way I set the table

Helping with my family.

(Substitute any family member or chore students suggest.)

Examples:

This is the way Daddy cooks the dinner . . .

This is the way Mommy takes out the trash . . .

This is the way Brother walks the dog . . .

This is the way Grandma fixes the car . . .

Family Jobs

For each student, fold a large piece of white paper in half in one direction, then again in the other direction, and then unfold it. The paper will now be divided into four sections. Ask students to draw a family member doing a job in each section. Have students write or dictate a sentence for each drawing.

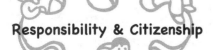

Responsibility & Citizenship

We Are Alike and Different

◉ Community Circle Activities ◉

Often a child's first exposure to a group outside the home is in a classroom. Building a warm, cooperative classroom community in which all members are valued and respected will go a long way toward putting students on the path toward good citizenship in the future. The activities in this chapter will help students explore and value diversity, as well as build common ground and work together. Young children entering preschool recognize roles and customs within their own families and may assume all families are similar. Children's cultural values, customs, and traditions from home should be nurtured and preserved to enable children to feel positive about themselves. At the same time, children need to learn about cultures which are different from their own in order to foster respect for others. The activities in this section will help students see the ways in which all children are similar while exploring and celebrating the ways in which every child is unique.

Pals Day

Once a week or so, have a Pals Day. Divide students into pairs and give each pair a copy of the Pals worksheet on page 101. Have each pair of "pals" find one thing that is alike about them and one thing that is different. Record the response by drawing and/or writing on their worksheet. Have each pair report on their comparisons. As the year progresses and students get used to this activity, you can have each pair find two or three things that are alike and different.

How We Are the Same

Tell students that you are going to describe someone in the class and they are going to guess who you are talking about. Tell students to listen carefully and to stand up if they hear something that is about them and sit down if they hear something that is not about them. Read the following aloud:

- You need food, water, and air to live.

- You need to sleep every night.

- You use the bathroom every day.

- You don't like it when your feelings get hurt.

- You like it when people are nice to you.

- You sweat when you get too hot and shiver when you get too cold.

- You have feelings. Sometimes you are happy and sometimes you are sad or afraid.

Empathy & Respect

Hopefully, all students (or most) will be standing. Point out to students that all the things you mentioned are things that are the same about all human beings. Even though we are different in many ways, we are the same in the most basic ways. Show students the We Are Alike mini poster on page 100, read the text aloud, and display it in the classroom. Make copies for each student to color and take home.

We Are Alike

- We need food, water, and air to live.

- We need to sleep every night.

- We use the bathroom every day.

- We sweat when we get too hot and shiver when we get too cold.

- We have feelings—sometimes we are happy and sometimes we are sad or afraid.

- We don't like it when our feelings get hurt.

- We like it when people are nice to us.

Pals

We are alike.

Pals

We are different.

We Are Alike and Different *(cont.)*

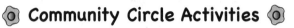

◎ Community Circle Activities ◎

Diversity Snack

At snack time, offer a plate of many different kinds of crackers and tell students that they can choose any three crackers that they would like, but they must wait to eat them. Once students have chosen their crackers, create a chart with the headings "Alike" and "Different." Have students list ways their crackers are alike (They are all crunchy; We can eat them) and ways they are different (They are different shapes; They have different colors). Point out to students that it is the same with people—people are alike in some ways, different in others, and having many different kinds makes life more interesting! Let students enjoy their snack.

> You will need crackers in several different shapes for this exercise.

Take a Poll

Make one copy of the I Like to...Poll on page 103 for each student. Have each student draw a picture of an activity that he or she enjoys (playing with a pet, reading books, eating ice cream, etc.). Then tell students to move around the room and talk with other students about what they enjoy. They should ask each person to sign his or her name on the right side and circle *yes* or *no* about the activity depicted. When all the signature lines on the poll are full, ask students to look at and discuss the results. Does everyone like to do the same things? Which activities do you enjoy? Who else likes the activities that you enjoy? Did you see any activities on another student's list that you might like to try?

Cooperation & Respect

Do you like it, too?

Yes　No

Yes　No

Yes　No

Yes　No

I Like To...

We Are Alike and Different (cont.)

Identity Culture

⊙ Community Circle Activities ⊙

Graphing Ways We Are Alike and Different

Use these graph questions to create a "Graph of the Day" about students. Graphs are a great way for students to see how they are like other students and how they are different.

- What is your favorite color?

- What is your favorite flavor of ice cream?

- Are you a boy or a girl?

- How do you get to school?

- What color are your eyes?

- What color is your hair?

- Which hand do you write with?

- What month is your birthday?

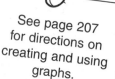

See page 207 for directions on creating and using graphs.

Respect

We Are Alike and Different *(cont.)*

◉ Community Circle Activities ◉

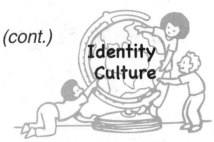

Identity
Culture

Venn Diagram

Lay two hula-hoops or large loops of yarn on the ground, overlapping to create a Venn diagram. Choose two attributes of the students in the group, for example brown hair and blue eyes, and label the graph (sentence strips work well).

Ask students with blue eyes to stand in the "Blue Eyes" hoop and students with brown hair to stand in the "Brown Hair" hoop. If there are any students who have blue eyes and brown hair, they should stand in the space where the two hoops overlap.

You will need two hula hoops or large loops of yarn for this activity.

When choosing attributes, remember that they should be two separate attributes that one student could possibly have. For example, blue eyes and brown eyes would not be good choices because no student can have both. To choose attributes, take a look at the students in the group and choose physical characteristics (hair color or length or style, eye color, freckles, boy or girl, etc.) or items of clothing (long or short sleeves, pants or skirt, types of shoes, etc.). You can expand the game to include talents and preferences

Blue Eyes

Brown Hair

Some Venn diagrams to try:

• "Freckles" and "Missing Teeth"

• "Braided Hair" and "Wears Glasses"

• "Eats Sandwich Crust" and "Curly Hair"

Compassion & Respect

We Are Alike and Different *(cont.)*

◉ Small Group Activities ◉

Identity
Culture

The Colors of Friendship

Set out multicultural tempera paints or pre-mix several skin tones from white, peach, brown, and black tempera paints. Mix each color with a drop of dish soap to make it easier to wash the paint off of skin later. Ask students to choose a paint color that matches their skin tone. Carefully place a dot of paint on the back of each student's hand and ask if it is a good match. If students say the paint does not match, help them mix colors in small containers to find a closer match. As each student creates his or her own special color, place the paint in a small jar with a lid and label it with the child's name.

When each student has a jar of his or her special color, discuss and compare the colors. Ask students to describe their colors—food-related words are often useful (apricot, wheat, honey, peach, cinnamon, caramel, chocolate, olive).

Help students paint one of their hands with their special color and make a handprint on construction paper. (Children may observe that some students' palms are a different shade than the backs of their hands.) Label with students' names. Display the handprints in the classroom with the caption "The Many Colors of Friendship."

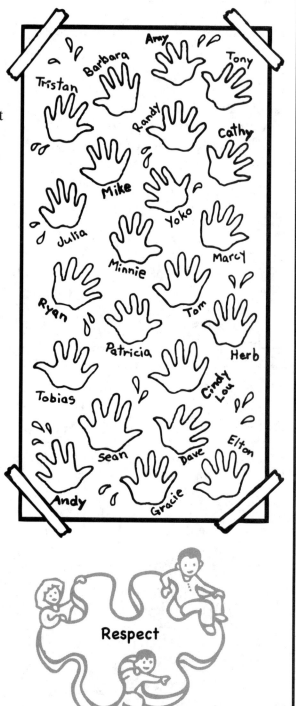

For this activity, you will need multicultural paints, small clear jars with lids, paintbrushes, soap, and construction paper.

Respect

We Are Alike and Different *(cont.)*
Community Circle Activities

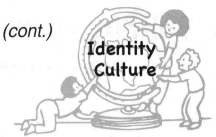

Identity Culture

Friendship Magnets

Select pieces from an unusable jigsaw puzzle that have roughly the shape of a human (head, two arms, two legs). You will need at least two pieces for each student. Have students choose two or more puzzle pieces and paint each using a different skin tone—they can share the colors they created in the Colors of Friendship activity (page 106). When dry, glue the pieces together so they look like they are holding hands (see illustration). Glue a magnet on the back.

For this craft, you will need old jigsaw puzzle pieces, skin tone paints (from the Colors of Friendship activity, page 106), and magnets.

Play Dough

Using the recipe on page 208, make several batches of play dough and give each one a distinct skin color. You may need to experiment with food coloring and spices (instead of drink mix) to create a few different colors (nutmeg and cinnamon work well and smell great, but be careful not to use too much of any one spice in the dough). Children can use gingerbread or cookie cutters to make people with the dough.

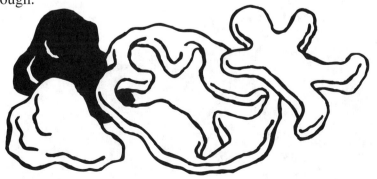

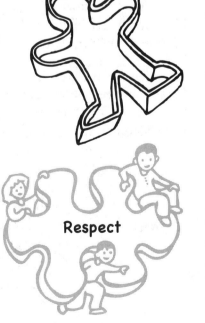

Respect

Building a Classroom Community

 Community Circle Activities

Relationships
Economics

Building a Classroom Community

It is important to develop a sense of community within a classroom. Young children need to learn to share, to take turns, and to treat each other with respect. Learning to work together and "play fair" isn't always easy—it takes time and it takes guidance. A classroom can be an excellent venue in which to practice these life skills. This chapter uses the tale of "The Little Red Hen" as a starting point for discussions and activities on the following topics:

Integrity & Responsibility　　　　　　**Cooperation & Fairness**

The Little Red Hen

Read aloud the story of "The Little Red Hen" (pages 109–110) and let your students decide the ending. Should Little Red Hen share the bread? Why or why not? This is a great opportunity to discuss cooperation and fairness.

Character figures on pages 111–113 can be made into felt board pieces or stick puppets for acting out the story. After the students have heard the story a few times, encourage them to act it out. Try different endings. How might the characters feel in each ending?

The Little Red Hen

Once upon a time, there was a little red hen that lived with a dog, a cat, and a pig. One day, Little Red Hen found some grains of wheat on the ground and decided to **plant** them. She asked her friends, "Who will help me plant this wheat?"

"Not I," said the dog.

"Not I," said the cat.

"Not I," said the pig.

"Then I'll do it myself," said Little Red Hen. And she did.

As the wheat was growing, it needed to be watered and the weeds needed to be pulled up. "Who will help me **tend** this wheat?" asked Little Red Hen.

"Not I," said the dog.

"Not I," said the cat.

"Not I," said the pig.

"Then I'll do it myself," said Little Red Hen. And she did.

When the wheat was tall and golden, it was time to cut it down. "Who will help me **harvest** this wheat?" asked Little Red Hen.

"Not I," said the dog.

"Not I," said the cat.

"Not I," said the pig.

"Then I'll do it myself," said Little Red Hen. And she did.

Once the wheat was cut, she needed to beat it to shake the grains out. "Who will help me **thresh** this wheat?" asked Little Red Hen.

"Not I," said the dog.

"Not I," said the cat.

"Not I," said the pig.

"Then I'll do it myself," said Little Red Hen. And she did.

Now the wheat needed to go to the **mill** to be ground into flour.

"Who will help me take this wheat to the mill?" asked Little Red Hen.

"Not I," said the dog.

"Not I," said the cat.

"Not I," said the pig.

"Then I'll do it myself," said Little Red Hen. And she did.

When Little Red Hen brought the flour home from the mill, she was ready to mix it with milk and butter and make bread. "Who will help me **make** the bread?" asked Little Red Hen.

"Not I," said the dog.

"Not I," said the cat.

"Not I," said the pig.

"Then I'll do it myself," said Little Red Hen. And she did.

Soon the wonderful smells of baking bread wafted through the air and when Little Red Hen took the bread out of the oven she called, "Who will help me **eat** this bread?"

"I will!" said the dog.

"I will!" said the cat.

"I will!" said the pig.

What do you think should happen now?

Building a Classroom Community *(cont.)*

◉ Community Circle Activities ◉

Relationships

Sharing: Friendship Fruit Salad

Ask each student to bring one piece of fruit from home. At school, let students wash and cut their fruit with a plastic knife and put everyone's fruit in a large bowl (depending on the students' developmental level, you may have to assist with the cutting). When the Friendship Fruit Salad is ready to eat, show students that everyone has contributed to the snack—the work has been shared. Talk about how to make sure each student gets a fair share of the salad. As the class is eating the fruit, talk about how they feel about sharing. How does it feel to get your fair share? How does it feel when you don't get as much as someone else? How does it feel when you get more than someone else? Why is it important to share?

Cooperation & Fairness

For this exercise you will need plastic knives, a large bowl, paper towels, and a regular knife and cutting board.

Cooperation: Partner Puzzles

Copy the Little Red Hen Puzzle (page 115) onto heavy cardstock (one copy for every two students) and cut apart the pieces. Divide the pieces of each puzzle into two groups and put each group in an envelope or plastic bag. Prepare enough puzzles in this way so that you have one puzzle for every two students.

Group students in pairs and give each pair of students a pair of puzzle bags. Tell students that they are to work together to assemble the puzzle, the only rule being that each student can only put the pieces from their own bag into the puzzle. When students have assembled their puzzles they can paste them onto a piece of paper and color the picture.

Afterward, discuss with students how they worked together and do a Looks Like/Sounds Like/Feels Like chart on page 123 for cooperation.

Cooperation & Fairness

Building a Classroom Community *(cont.)*

Community Circle Activities

Responsibility

Kindness: The Kindness Jar

Decorate (or have students decorate) a large jar to be the class Kindness Jar. Make copies of the Kindness Slips on page 117 and cut them apart. Set them next to the Kindness Jar in a place that students can easily access during the day.

Show students the jar and tell them that this will be the class "Kindness Jar." Show students the slips and tell them that at any point during the day if someone is kind to them they can fill out a slip by writing or dictating to an adult and put it in the jar. With students, brainstorm a list of ways they can be kind to others. At the end of every day, read the Kindness Slips aloud to the class and cheer for everyone who has been kind.

Kindness

You will need a large jar with a lid for this activity.

Empathy: How Does It Feel?

Young children are often just beginning to learn empathy, which is a necessary first step toward getting along with others. Provide some group practice by showing students the illustrations on pages 118–121 and reading the text aloud. Ask students to talk about how the characters in each situation are feeling. Help students expand their vocabulary by introducing words like proud, grateful, embarrassed, guilty, disappointed, kind, surprised, and relieved.

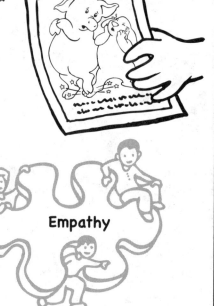

Empathy

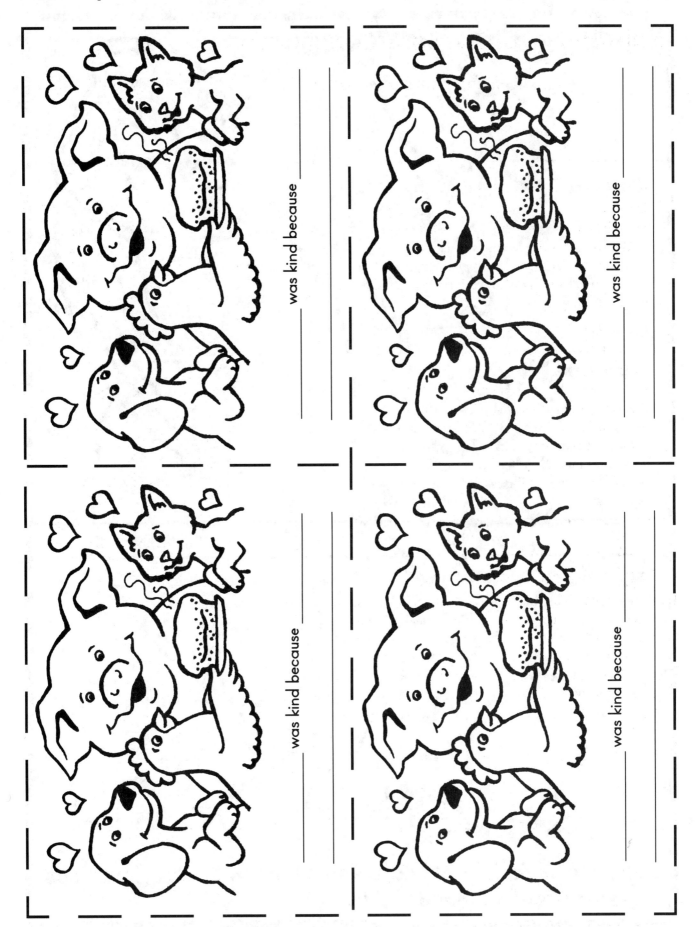

The pig is taking bread away from the cat. How does the cat feel? How does the pig feel?

Little Red Hen is sharing her bread with the other animals. How does Little Red Hen feel? How do the other animals feel?

**The pig has accidentally stepped on the dog's paw.
How does the pig feel? How does the dog feel?**

Little Red Hen has dropped her flour on the ground and the dog is helping her clean it up. How does Little Red Hen feel? How does the dog feel?

Building a Classroom Community *(cont.)*

◎ Community Circle Activities ◎

**Civics
Relationships
Economics**

Working Together

Now that students have learned about working together, give them practice in cooperating with others toward reaching a common goal. By providing opportunities for group jobs and helping students understand the process, each student will begin to feel he or she is an important and needed member of the classroom community. Big jobs can be done by the whole class while smaller jobs may require a smaller group of students.

Begin by explaining the job to students, then leading a discussion about how they can work together. You may also want to do a Looks Like/Sounds Like/Feels Like chart (page 123).

- What, exactly, do you need to do?

- Will you need tools or equipment to do the job?

- Will you break the job into parts for each person or will everyone be doing the same thing?

- How will you know when you are finished?

While students are working, an adult should be present to answer questions and supervise for safety, but the students should be in charge of the project.

After students decide that they have completed the job, gather them for a review.

- How did it go? Did everyone do his or her part?

- Did you reach your goal? How do you know?

- How do you feel about the job that you did?

- Would you do anything differently next time?

Sample cooperative jobs:

- Put away the materials for an activity center and set up a new one.

- Clean up the sand or water table area.

- Rearrange the block shelves.

- Prepare the class snack.

- Clean the cage of a class pet.

- Rake leaves on the playground.

- Put away or get out the playground toys.

Self-discipline & Responsibility

Building a Classroom Community *(cont.)*  Civics Relationships

 Community Circle Activities

Looks Like/Sounds Like/Feels Like

Abstract ideas such as cooperation and kindness can be difficult for young children to understand. Also, students often need specific instructions for doing jobs in the classroom. This chart can help make abstract ideas more concrete and jobs more child-friendly by talking about what they *look like*, *sound like*, and *feel like*.

This chart can be used to analyze expected behaviors, classroom rules, jobs that need to be done in the classroom, or character traits. Create a three-column chart with the subheadings "Looks Like," "Sounds Like," "Feels Like" (see example below). Give the chart a title. Ask students to talk about what it looks like (what people do), what it sounds like (what people say) and what it feels like (how it makes them feel). You can also have students act out or role play each idea.

Putting Away Blocks

Looks Like. . .	Sounds Like. . .	Feels Like. . .
One person picks up blocks and hands them to another	Soft sounds of blocks being set on shelves	
placing blocks gently on the shelf	polite words—please, thank you	proud calm
blocks are stacked neatly	"Here you go." Could you please hand me that long block?"	like we did a good job

Sharing

Looks Like. . .	Sounds Like. . .	Feels Like. . .
dividing something equally in half	"May I have a turn please?"	happy
taking turns	"Would you like some?"	proud
making sure everyone has their fair share	"Thank you!"	grateful

Classroom Rules
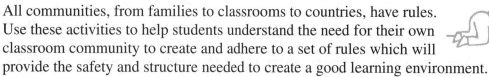
◉ Community Circle Activities ◉

All communities, from families to classrooms to countries, have rules. Use these activities to help students understand the need for their own classroom community to create and adhere to a set of rules which will provide the safety and structure needed to create a good learning environment.

Our Class Rules!

Discuss with your class what the word "rule" means. Ask students to name some rules that they have at home. Explain that classroom rules help everyone stay safe and get along so that they can all learn and have fun.

Create a chart with two columns headed "Rule" and "Reason." Ask students to name some of the classroom and playground rules and record them in the first column. Then, for each rule, talk about why that rule is important and record students' reasons in the second column. Post this important chart in the classroom and refer to it often.

Why We Have Our Class Rules	
Rule	**Why we have that rule...**
Raise your hand to speak	So everyone is not talking at the same time
Push in your chair	So no one will trip over it
Walk, don't run	So you won't bump into anyone and you won't fall
Keep your hands to yourself	So you won't hurt someone else
Put away toys	So no one will trip over them and next time we can find them

Rule Books

- Have students draw illustrations of themselves following the rules to create a book of classroom rules.

- Have students write or tell a story about someone who didn't follow rules.

Classroom Rules *(cont.)*

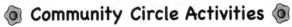

◉ **Community Circle Activities** ◉

Civics

Types of Rules

Some rules are for safety, others demonstrate respect and caring for others. Make copies of the symbols on page 126 and cut them out. With students, go through your class rules list and ask students identify whether each rule is a rule to keep them safe (safety rule) or a rule that helps them get along and respect each other (respect rule). Using a glue stick, place a safety alert symbol by the safety rules and a heart symbol by the respect rules.

You will need glue sticks and the cutout symbols found on page 126.

Is It Safe? Safety Rule Review

For a quick safety rule review each day, give students some examples of classroom behavior and have them respond with a "thumbs up" for safe behaviors and "thumbs down" for unsafe behaviors. The worksheet on page 127 will provide extra practice. Ask students to look at each picture and circle the "thumbs up" if the picture shows a student doing something safe and "thumbs down" if the picture shows an unsafe behavior. Follow up with a discussion of why each behavior is safe or unsafe and ask students how they would correct the unsafe behaviors.

Responsibility & Citizenship

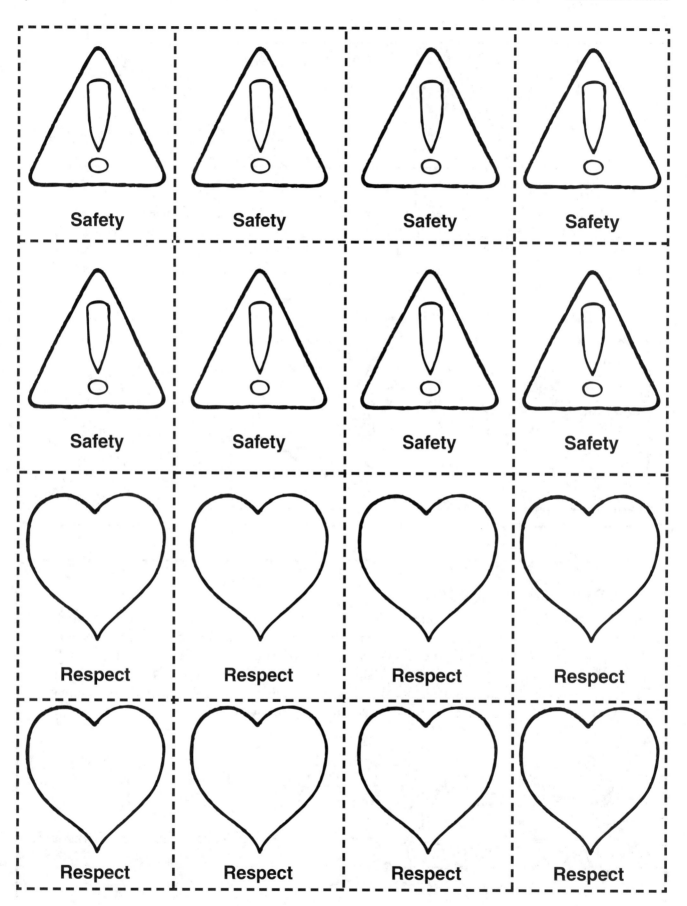

Is It Safe? Worksheet

Directions: Circle "thumbs up" if the activity is safe and "thumbs down" if the activity is not safe.

Classroom Rules *(cont.)*

 Small Group Activities

Relationships & Civics

Making New Rules

Wrap a new classroom item as a gift. Try a picture book, a set of manipulatives, a tool for the housekeeping corner, or any other item that students will want to use. Present the gift to the class. Have a class discussion about the use of the new item, helping students understand that it belongs to the class and must be shared. Ask students to brainstorm possible rules about using the new item. As a group, evaluate all the suggested rules and help students choose a set of rules that they think will work.

You will need a gift-wrapped classroom item for this exercise.

Discussion Questions

- How many people can use it at once?
- How long does each person or group need to use it?
- How can we decide who gets to use it when?
- How can we be sure there is no fighting over the new item?
- How can we settle arguments about who gets to use it?

After a period of time, evaluate the effectiveness of the chosen rules. Ask students if each of the rules is working as they intended. As a group, change or modify any rules as needed.

It's My Turn!

One of the rules that applies not only to the classroom but to communities in general is taking turns. Ask students to think of times that their parents have to wait their turn (in line at the grocery store, stopping at a stop sign, etc.). Talk with students about the different ways to decide whose turn it is to do something. Some they may be familiar with are:

- lining up

- raising your hand

- Eenie, Meenie, Miney, Moe

- Rock, Paper, Scissors

Fairness & Cooperation

- One Potato, Two Potato

Divide students into small groups and ask each group to create a new way to determine the order in which each child gets a turn at an activity.

School Helpers

◉ **Small Group Activities** ◉

Meet the Helpers

It is important for students to become familiar with all of the adults working at your school so that they can distinguish between school helpers and strangers. Take students on a tour of your campus to meet office staff, cafeteria workers, librarians, custodians, and anyone else students may come in contact with. Be sure to let the staff know you are coming and what you will be doing. Have students greet staff members politely ("*Good Morning, Mr. Jones!*") and ask them to tell students a bit about their jobs. Bring a camera and take pictures of each helper.

Mount the pictures you took of school helpers on a poster or put them in a book and label each with the school helper's name and title. Help students remember who they saw on the tour by showing the photos and asking them to identify all of the helpers and describe their jobs. Write students' job descriptions next to the photos.

You will need a camera for this activity.

Thank You!

Divide students into small groups and have each group create a "thank you" card for one of the school helpers you visited.

You will need card stock and art supplies for this activity.

School Helpers *(cont.)*

⚙ Small Group Activities ⚙

Who Can Help?

Using the photos from your school tour, play "Who Can Help?" Give examples of situations that could happen at school and ask students to choose the picture of the person that could help.

For this exercise, you will need the pictures taken during your school tour!

Who can help you if . . .

- you get lost at school?

- you have to take something to the office?

- you want to buy lunch?

- you want to check a book out from the library?

- you feel sick on the bus?

- someone spilled something in the hall?

- you want to cross the street?

- you fall and skin your knee?

- someone is picking on you on the playground?

Helper Role Play

Have students role play interactions with adult helpers at school. Describe a situation that students might encounter at school (see examples in Who Can Help? above) and ask students which adult helper would be involved. Ask for student volunteers to play both the student and the adult. As they perform, ask the class to observe and give "thumbs up" when the students demonstrate polite behaviors, such as using "please" and "thank you."

Respect

Classroom Geography

⊚ Community Circle Activities ⊚

Geography

Building a Map

On chart paper draw a simple outline of your circle time area — a simple rectangle, circle, or square will do. Tell students that they are going to help you make a map of the circle-time area. Explain that a map is a picture which shows a place as if you were looking down on it from up above. Ask students to imagine that they are up on the ceiling, looking down onto the circle-time area.

Write your name on a sticky note and place it on the map to show where you sit. Next, name a student who sits close to you and show where that student should be on the map, then have that student write his or her name on a sticky note and place it in the correct spot. Continue until all students have added their names to the map.

Display your map in the classroom and use it to practice map reading skills. Ask students to identify individuals as you give directional clues; "This person sits in front of Randy and next to Kathryn," or "I am thinking of a student who sits in the bottom, left corner of the map." If you need to reassign seats, use the map to show students their new spots.

> If you don't have a circle time area, use student desk or table assignments.

> You will need chart paper, markers, and sticky notes for this activity.

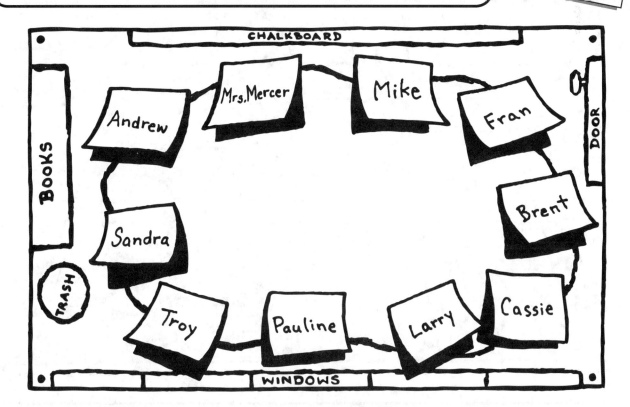

Classroom Geography *(cont.)*

⚙ Community Circle Activities ⚙

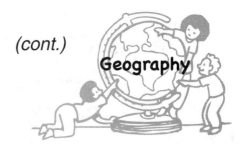
Geography

Block Map

Use building blocks to create a model, or three-dimensional map, of your school. Begin by taking students on a walking tour of the school, observing and discussing the sizes and positions of different buildings and landmarks as you go. Back in the classroom, roughly mark the outline shape of the campus and any pathways or hallways between buildings using blue painter's tape (it removes easily) on the floor or on a large table. Have students choose blocks to represent buildings, lunch tables, play equipment, and any other large landmarks and place them on the map. Once students think they have completed the model, take them back out for a second look at the campus—they may notice things they missed the first time. Back in class, have them make any needed adjustments to their model.

If you don't have blocks, empty cardboard boxes, tissue boxes, and containers will work.

You will need blocks and blue painter's tape for this activity. You will also need toys.

Classroom Geography *(cont.)*
◉ Community Circle Activities ◉

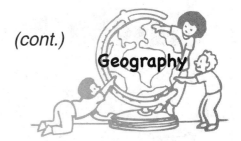

Goldilocks Story Map

Copy the map on page 136 for each student. Make a paper Goldilocks marker and a Three Bears marker for each student (page 137). Attach craft sticks to the back of the markers. (See below.)

Explain to students that this is a map of the events in the story of "Goldilocks and the Three Bears." Give each student a Goldilocks marker and a Three Bears marker. Read the story aloud slowly, and ask students to move their Goldilocks and Three Bears around the map along with the story. Monitor students to see that they are following directions.

Set out some maps and "Goldilocks and Three Bears" markers at a center and let students practice acting out the story.

Try making story maps with other familiar stories such as "Little Red Riding Hood," "The Gingerbread Man," and "The Three Billy Goats Gruff."

Goldilocks and the Three Bears

Once upon a time, there were three bears who lived in the woods: a great, big Papa Bear, a middle-sized Mama Bear, and a wee little Baby Bear. *(Put the bears in their house.)*

One morning Mama Bear made some porridge, but it was too hot to eat, so the bears went for a walk in the woods while it cooled. *(Put the bears in the woods.)*

Along came a little girl named Goldilocks. She saw the bears' house and wondered who lived there. *(Put Goldilocks outside the house.)*

Goldilocks went up to the door and knocked, but no one answered so she walked right in. *(Move Goldilocks into the front hall of the house.)*

Goldilocks smelled something yummy, so she went into the kitchen. *(Move Goldilocks into the kitchen.)*

At the table in the kitchen, there were three bowls of porridge.

She tried the porridge in the great big bowl.

"This porridge is too hot!" she exclaimed.

So she tried the porridge in the medium-sized bowl.

"This porridge is too cold," she said

So she tried the porridge in the wee little bowl.

"Ahhh, this porridge is just right," she said, and she ate it all up.

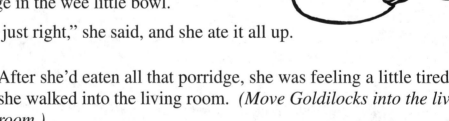

After she'd eaten all that porridge, she was feeling a little tired, so she walked into the living room. *(Move Goldilocks into the living room.)*

In the living room were three chairs.

Goldilocks sat in the great big chair and said, "This chair is too hard!"

Goldilocks sat in the middle-sized chair and said, "This chair is too soft!"

So she sat in the wee little chair and said, "Ahhh, this chair is just right."

But she was too big for the little chair and it fell to pieces!

Goldilocks was getting sleepy, so she went upstairs to the bedroom. *(Move Goldilocks up the stairs and into the bedroom.)*

She lay down on the great big bed and said, "This bed is too hard!"

Then she lay down on the middle-sized bed and said, "This bed is too soft!"

Then she lay down on the wee little bed and said, "Ahhh, this bed is just right."

Goldilocks fell fast asleep. *(Put Goldilocks in the little bed.)*

As Goldilocks was sleeping, the three bears came home. *(Put the bears in the front hall.)*

They went into the kitchen to eat their breakfast. *(Move the bears to the kitchen.)*

"Someone's been eating my porridge," growled Papa Bear.

"Someone's been eating my porridge," said Mama Bear.

"Someone's been eating my porridge, and they ate it all up!" cried Baby Bear.

The bears went into the living room.

(Move the bears to the living room.)

"Someone's been sitting in my chair," growled the Papa Bear.

"Someone's been sitting in my chair," said Mama Bear.

"Someone's been sitting in my chair and it's broken all to pieces," cried Baby Bear.

The bears went upstairs to the bedroom. *(Move the bears up the stairs and into the bedroom.)*

"Someone's been sleeping in my bed," growled Papa Bear.

"Someone's been sleeping in my bed," said Mama Bear.

"Someone's been sleeping in my bed and she's still there!" cried Baby Bear.

Just then, Goldilocks woke up and saw the three bears. She screamed, jumped up, and ran out of the room. Goldilocks ran down the stairs, opened the door, and ran away into the forest.

(Take Goldilocks down the stairs, out the door, and into the forest.)

And Goldilocks learned never to go into someone's home unless she was invited!

THE END

Goldilocks

Goldilocks

The Three Bears

The Three Bears

Goldilocks

Goldilocks

The Three Bears

The Three Bears

Classroom Geography (cont.)

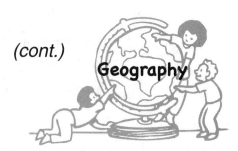

Geography

✿ Community Circle Activities ✿

Treasure Hunt Map

Get Ready

Hide some "treasure" around the playground for students to find—it can be small toys, blocks, plastic coins, snacks, or anything you like. Create a simple map of the treasure hunt area, drawing in the basic shapes and labeling any major landmarks (swings, slide, tables, trees, etc.). You will be splitting your class into small groups—make one copy of the map for each group. Indicate different treasure hiding places on each map so that each group is looking for a different set of treasure. This eliminates competition so students are focused on their map, not the other teams. You will want to have at least one piece of treasure for every student. You can mark the hiding spots with a colored "X" or a star—making the marks a bright color will help students see them.

Get Set

Give a map to each group and ask them to look it over and discuss it. Ask if they know what area the map represents and what the colored marks might be. Go over each landmark on the map so students have a clear understanding of where everything is.

You will need copies of a simple map of your playground or play area.

Go

Let students find their treasure! Once each group has found their treasure, have them split it up fairly among the members of the group. Discuss how students used the maps. If any treasure has not been found, have the entire class analyze the map to find it.

Community Economics

◉ Community Circle Activities ◉

Economics

While young children are naturally focused on their own small worlds, we can begin to expand their experiences. The activities in this chapter will help students look beyond their homes, families, and classrooms by focusing on their interactions with their communities, our country, and our Earth.

Wants and Needs

Prepare a piece of chart paper with two columns headed "Needs" and "Wants." Introduce the terms *need* and *want* to students. Explain that there are some things we need—we cannot live without them. A child's needs include air, food, water, clothing, shelter, and the care of a loving adult. There are many other things that we want—things like toys, television, and cookies, but we could survive without them. Ask students to give you examples of wants and needs—discuss each and record them on the chart paper.

Point out to students that needs are things that they must have to survive. Their families must make sure they have these things before they can get any of the things they want.

Wants and Needs Practice

Copy the Wants Cards on page 140 (one card for each student) onto yellow paper. Copy the Needs Cards on page 141 (one card for each student) onto red paper. Make one copy of each Item Card on pages 142–153 for yourself.

Give each student one red Need Card and one yellow Want Card. Tell students that as you show them some pictures, they should hold up the red card if the picture shows something they need and the yellow card if the picture shows something they want. As you hold up and name each card, have students hold up either their needs or wants cards. If the vote is not unanimous, discuss the item.

You will need red and yellow copy paper for this activity.

Self-discipline & Fairness

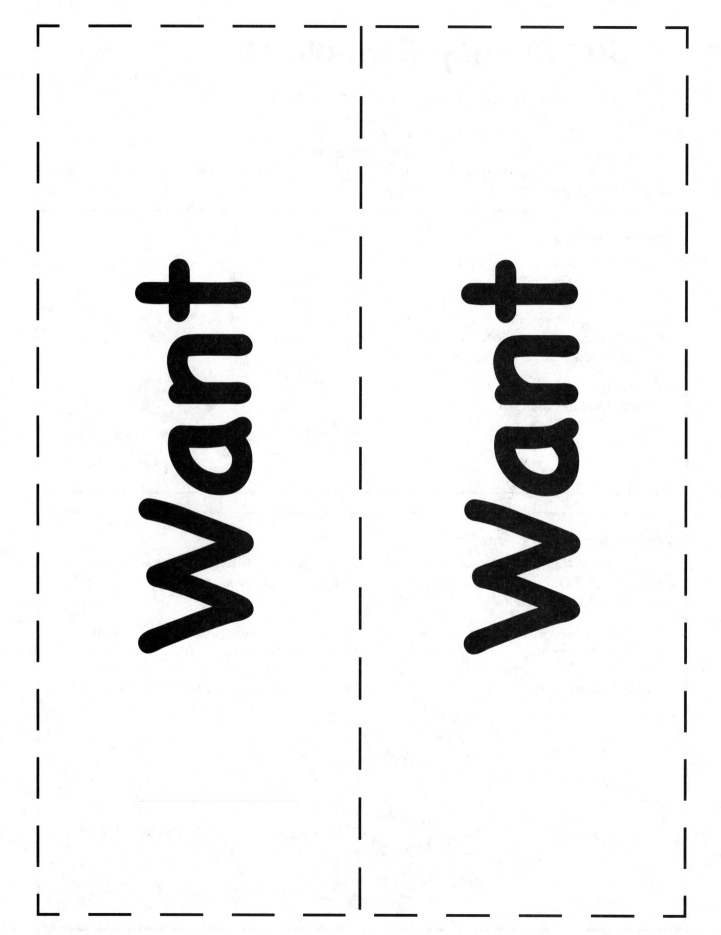

Need

Need

dinner

video game

house

birthday cake

doll

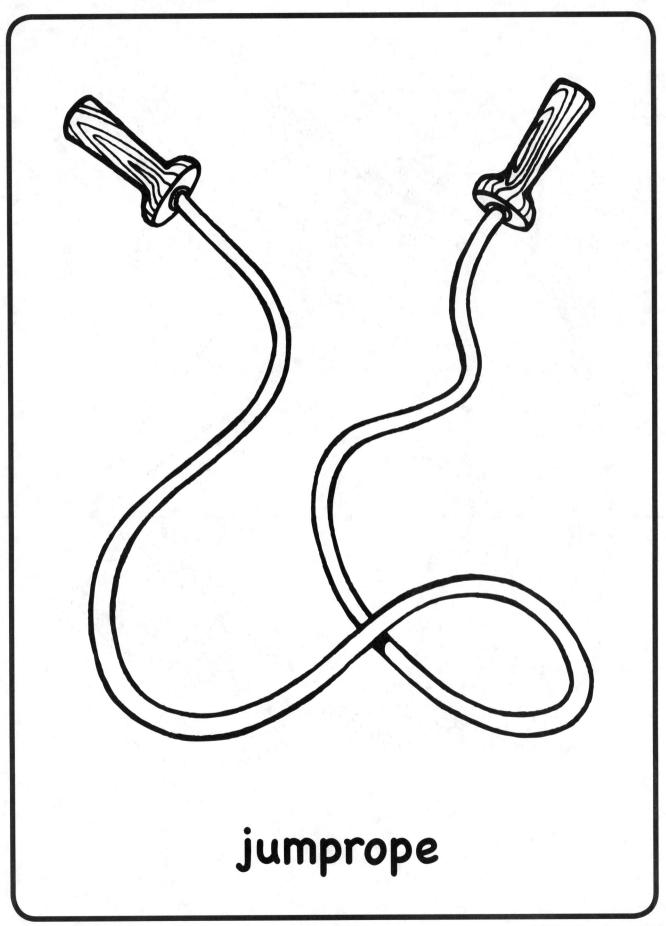

jumprope

jacket

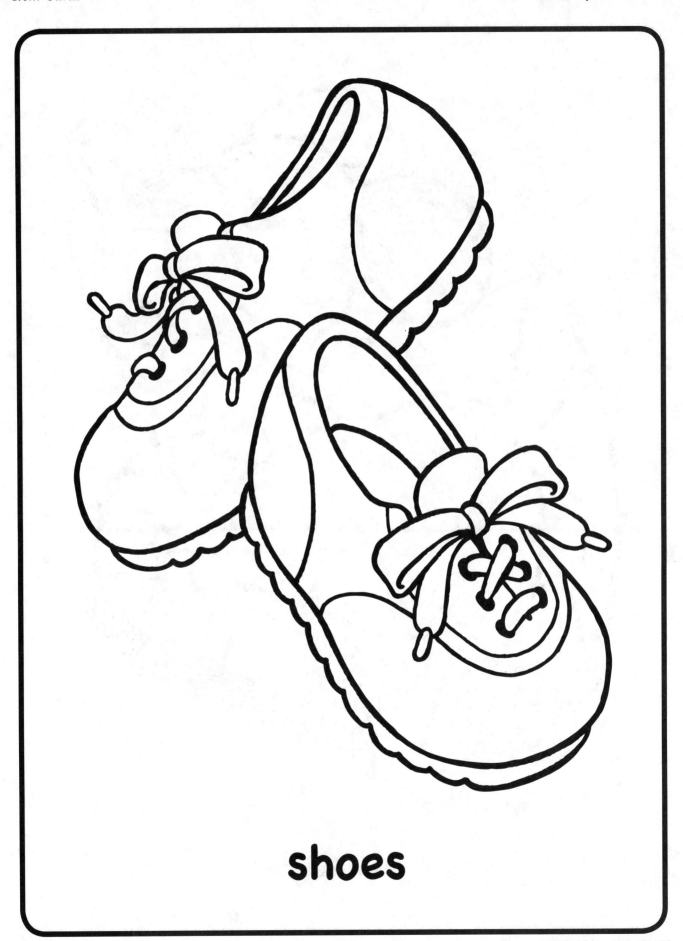

shoes

puppy

breakfast

book

dentist

Community Economics *(cont.)*

Economics

🔘 Community Circle Activities 🔘

Wants and Needs Book

Copy the Wants and Needs Worksheet (on page 155) for each student. Ask students to illustrate a want on one half of the paper and a need on the other half. Have students dictate or write a sentence for each drawing. Gather the pages into a class book about wants and needs.

Filling Wants and Needs

Now that students know the difference between a want and a need, talk about how they fulfill those wants and needs in their community. Hold up each Item Card (on pages 142–153) and ask students how they would fulfill that want or need.

Examples

- **Book** — You could buy it at the bookstore, borrow it from the library, or borrow it from a friend.
- **Dinner** — Your parents could buy food at the grocery store and make it; you could go to a restaurant and buy it.
- **Shoes** — Your parents could buy them for you at a store; you could buy them at a yard sale; you could get them from an older brother, sister, or cousin.

Filling Wants and Needs Worksheet

Students can practice matching wants and needs to the places they can be found with the worksheet on page 156.

Self-discipline

I need

I want

Wants and Needs

Draw a line from the item that you might want or need to the place where you could get it. Circle the things that you *need*.

Items   ## Places

Community Economics *(cont.)*

Economics

Where Does It Come From?

Copy and assemble the Where Does Milk Come From? minibook on pages 158–161 for each student. Remind students that one of their needs is food. Where in the community do they get food (grocery store, restaurant)? Do they know where the food comes from and how it gets to the store?

Read the Where Does Milk Come From? minibook along with students. Let them color the books and take them home to share with their families. Encourage students to find out more about where the things they buy come from.

Classroom Economy

Set up a store in your classroom. Provide small items for students to "sell" and some play money. A toy cash register and some old purses and wallets will make the experience even more realistic. Be sure everyone knows that the store is just for practice and that at the end of every day all of the goods and money should be back in the store. Encourage students to expand on the idea—maybe someone wants to start a library with a checkout system, a doll hospital, or a tricycle repair business on the playground.

Where Does Milk Come From?

Name: _____

This is a dairy farmer. This is a dairy cow.

1

The farmer uses machines to milk the cows on his dairy farm.

2

A tanker truck takes the milk to a factory.

3

Special machines make sure the milk is safe and put it into containers.

Milk is also used to make cheese, butter, and ice cream. **5**

Trucks bring the milk and milk products to your store.

People buy and eat milk products. 7

Community Helpers

◉ **Community Circle Activities** ◉

Who Are Community Helpers?

Make one copy of each of the Community Helper mini posters on pages 163–168.

Review with students the ways in which adults help them at home and at school. (See School Helpers on pages 129 and 130.) Ask if students can think of any other adults who help them. Record students' answers on chart paper and title the list "Community Helpers."

Show each Community Helper mini poster to students and read the text aloud. If any of the helpers are not on the class chart, add them and discuss how those people help in the community.

Community Helpers Song

Copy and display the mini poster on page 169 and teach students a song about community helpers. Invite students to make up their own additional verses about other helpers.

Community Helper Matching Worksheets

Provide practice in matching community helpers to tools they use and to hats used in specific jobs with the worksheets on pages 170 and 171.

Community Helpers Fill Wants and Needs

Copy the cards on pages 172–173 and cut apart. You may want to color them and laminate them for durability.

Have students match each child with a need or a want to the community helper who can help him or her fill it.

Police Officers

Fire Fighters

Police officers keep us safe by making sure everyone follows the law.

Fire fighters keep us safe by preventing and putting out fires.

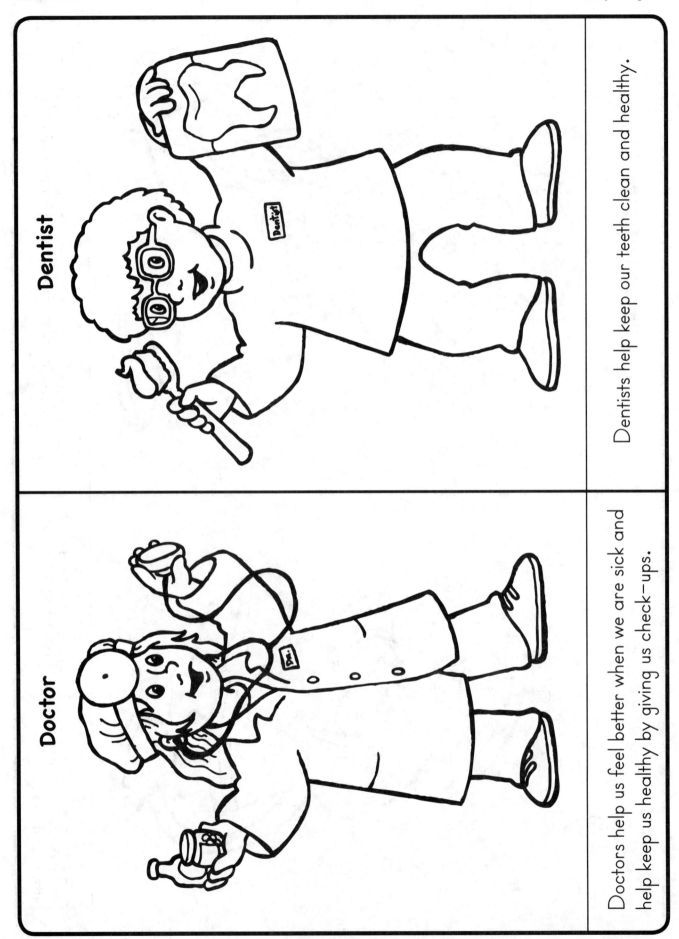

Dentist

Dentists help keep our teeth clean and healthy.

Doctor

Doctors help us feel better when we are sick and help keep us healthy by giving us check-ups.

Veterinarian

Veterinarians take care of our animals.

Farmer

Farmers grow good food for us to eat.

Highway Construction Worker

Highway construction workers fix our roads and keep them safe to drive on.

Sanitation Worker

Sanitation workers take away all our trash.

Bus Driver

Crossing Guard

Bus drivers take us safely where we need to go.

Crossing guards help us cross the street safely.

Community Helpers Song

(Try to sing to the tune of "London Bridge")

Firefighters put out fires,
put out fires, put out fires
Firefighters put out fires
They are community helpers.

Doctors help to make us well,
make us well, make us well
Doctors help to make us well
They are community helpers.

Teachers help us learn and grow,
learn and grow, learn and grow
Teachers help us learn and grow
They are community helpers.

Crossing guards make sure we're safe,
sure we're safe, sure we're safe
Crossing guards make sure we're safe,
They are community helpers.

Mail carriers bring us mail,
bring us mail, bring us mail
Mail carriers bring us mail
They are community helpers.

Community Helpers Matching

Directions: Draw a line to match each community helper to something he or she uses at work.

Community Helpers	Tools

Community Helpers Hat Matching

Directions: Cut out the hats and paste them on the correct community helpers.

doctor

mail carrier

sanitation worker

crossing guard

librarian

veterinarian

Community Helpers (cont.)

◉ Small Group Activities ◉

Civics

Community Helper Dress-Up Center

Put together some dress-up boxes so students can pretend to be community helpers. Label each box with the name of the helper and let students dress up during free choice time or center time.

- **Chef:** Chef's hat (called a toque), apron, mixing bowls, spoons and whisks
- **Firefighter:** hat, boots, raincoat, hose
- **Doctor:** white lab coat, stethoscope, doctor kit
- **Construction Worker:** hard hat, tools, boots, safety goggles
- **Mail Carrier:** hat, mail bag, envelopes, junk mail
- **Police Officer:** hat, radio, badge

You will need costume uniforms for this activity.

Mail Bags

Help students make mail bags and play postal carrier. Put two large pieces of construction paper together and punch holes around three sides. Help students lace yarn through the holes, leaving the top open. Add a yarn handle and write "US Mail" on the bag. Provide junk mail or used envelopes for the mail carriers to pick up and deliver.

You will need construction paper and yarn for this activity.

Fight that Fire!

Draw flames on the side of a school building or on the blacktop or sidewalk with washable, colored chalk. Let students play firefighter and put the fire out with water-filled squirt bottles!

You will need colored chalk and squirt bottles for this activity.

Leadership

○ **Community Circle Activities** ○

**Civics
Relationships**

Leaders

Fill in the blanks in the Leaders minibook on pages 176–177. Copy and assemble the filled-in minibook for each student. Provide half sheets of construction paper for students to make covers for the minibooks.

To begin, play a few quick games of "Red Light, Green Light" or "Simon Says." Let several students have a turn to be the leader. Afterward, ask students to think about the role of a leader. How does someone become a leader? What makes a good leader? Have students think about other games they play on the playground—do any of the games have a leader?

Ask students:

- Who is (or are) the leader(s) in your home? (Mother, father, or other adult)

- Who is the leader in our classroom? (The teacher)

- Who is the leader of our school? (The principal)

- Tell students that some of our community helpers are leaders. Some lead small groups, like a classroom, and some lead very large groups, like an entire country.

- Read the Leaders minibook (pages 176–177) to students and give them each a copy to color and take home.

Citizenship

A teacher is the leader of a classroom.

My teacher is _____.

We are in Room _____.

A principal is the leader of a school.

My school is called_____.

A mayor is the leader of a town.

My town is called _____.

A governor is the leader of a state.

My state is _____.

The president is the leader of our country.

My country is_____.

Leadership *(cont.)*

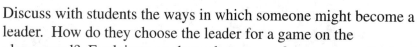 Community Circle Activities

Discuss with students the ways in which someone might become a leader. How do they choose the leader for a game on the playground? Explain to students that some of our community leaders, like mayors, governors, and presidents, are elected. That means that the people they will be leading vote to choose their leader. Who votes for a mayor? Who votes for a governor? Who votes for the President?

Get Out the Vote!

Discuss the rules of elections:

- Every person gets one vote.
- No one can tell anyone else how to vote—everyone makes up his or her own mind.
- Voting is secret—you don't have to tell who or what you voted for unless you want to.
- The person (or thing) that gets the most votes wins.

Hold an election to choose the class' favorite pet.

- Copy the ballots on page 179 for each student.
- Have students decorate an empty box to create a ballot box.
- Have student volunteers pass out the ballots, making sure that each student only gets one ballot.
- Show students how to fill out their ballots by marking only one box. Tell them that if they mark more than one pet, their ballot will not be counted. If their favorite pet is not on the ballot, they may write it in on the blank line. Remind them that they should NOT put their names on the ballots.
- When voting is completed, have student volunteers count the ballots in front of the class and tally the votes on chart paper. Write "Our favorite pet is…" on the chart paper and display it in the classroom.

Practice the concept of voting many times during the school year. At story time, have students vote on which book to read. At snack time, give students a choice of two snacks to vote on. Practice different forms of voting:

- Raise your hand (eyes closed!)
- Fill out a ballot
- Put a small object in a jar

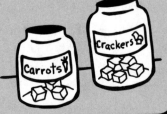

Integrity & Citizenship

Our Favorite Pet Ballot

dog

cat

bird

fish

hamster

_____ write-in vote

My Place in the World

◉ Community Circle Activities ◉

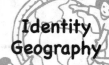

Identity
Geography

Where I Live

Display for the class a map that encompasses the areas where students live. Alternatively, you could draw a simple outline map on large chart paper or butcher paper. Help each student place a sticker or sticky note with his or her name and address to mark the place where he or she lives. As a group, mark places that students go, such as your school, grocery stores, parks, and libraries with a highlighter. Let students "walk" their fingers around the map or "drive" small toy cars to show routes from their homes to different places of interest.

You will need a local map, a highlighter, and sticky notes for this activity.

Where I Live Minibook

Copy and complete the Where I Live minibook (on pages 182–184) for each student. Complete the book with students. Let students color the book individually. Practice reading it aloud together.

Our Earth

Explain that the Earth is shaped somewhat like a ball, with land and water covering it. Show students how land and water are depicted on the globe. Sit students in a circle and roll the globe to each student. As each student catches it, have him or her state whether his or her hands are touching water or land.

Next, show students a world map and explain that this is a way of looking at all the land and water on Earth all at once, by laying it out flat. Even though the Earth is not really flat, the map allows us to see everything on Earth at the same time. Practice finding the continents on both the globe and the world map.

You will need a world map and a globe for this activity.

My Place in the World (cont)

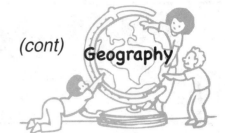

Geography

@ Community Circle Activities @

My Place in the World

Show students the map they created in Where I Live (page 180) or a map of their local area. Ask them to come up close to the map. What details can they see? Can they find houses, roads, stores, parks? Now, ask students to take five large steps back from the map. Can they still see all the details? Ask students to take more steps back until they are as far from the map as the classroom will allow. Can they still see the details? Help them verbalize that everything looks smaller on the map as they move farther away from it.

- Ask students to imagine that they are in the Space Shuttle (or a rocket ship), blasting off from Earth and heading into outer space. Ask them to pretend they are looking out the window of the shuttle as you hold up the local map. Can they see their school?

- Flip to the state map, telling students that they are high enough now to see the whole state. As you move the map farther away from them, ask students to keep looking out the shuttle window. What can they see now? Can they still see their school or their town?

- Flip to the U.S. map, telling students that now they can see the whole country. As you slowly move the map farther away from students, ask if the country looks larger or smaller as they get farther away. Can they still see their state or their town?

- Now, switch to the globe. Tell students that they can see the whole Earth now! Can they see their country or their state any more? Point out the continent of North America.

- Turn the globe slowly. Tell students that they are orbiting, or going around, the Earth. Ask them to describe what they see.

- Now reverse the entire process as the Shuttle comes in for a safe landing.

You will need flipchart paper, a local, a state, a U.S. map and a globe for this activity. Paste each map on the flipchart.

Where I Live

This is my home. My street address is

_____. ①

The name of my town is _____.

My state is part of the United States of America. The name
of my state is _____. ③

The U.S.A. is on a continent called North America.

North America is on the planet Earth.

My Country

⬡ Community Circle Activities ⬡

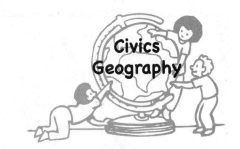

Civics
Geography

Familiar Symbols

Make one copy of each American Symbols mini poster on pages 186–189. Color the illustrations if desired. Copy and assemble the minibook (pages 190–192) for each student.

Explain to students that the name of our country is the United States of America. Sometimes we shorten the name to America or the U.S.A. Show students a map of the United States and explain that our country is made up of fifty states and that most fit together like the pieces of a puzzle.

Tell students that our country has many symbols. A symbol is a picture or thing that stands for something else. Remind students of the symbols they used to mark the class rules either a "safety rule" or a "respect rule" on page 125. Show students the American symbols mini poster on page 186 and discuss what each symbol means.

Show students each of the American Symbols mini posters (pages 186–189) and read the text under each symbol aloud.

American Symbols Minibook

Read the American Symbols minibook on pages 190–192 to students, then give each student a copy to color and take home.

Our Flag

With students, closely inspect the American flag. How many stripes are there? Is the top stripe red or white? Which corner do the blue field and stars go in?

Copy the flag on page 193 for each student and have them color it.

For a more hands-on activity, give students a large rectangle of white construction paper, some red strips cut to the length of the white paper, a blue rectangle cut to size, and a sheet of star stickers. Let students assemble a paper flag, using the real flag for reference.

You will need an American flag, sheets of red, white, and blue construction paper, and small star stickers for this activity.

Citizenship

Familiar Symbols

Other names for the American flag are "The Red, White, and Blue," "The Stars and Stripes," and "Old Glory."

Red, white, and blue are the colors of the United States of America. Our flag has thirteen red and white stripes and fifty white stars on a blue rectangle.

Where have you seen an American Flag?

When you say the Pledge of Allegiance you show respect for America. You put your right hand over your heart, stand up straight, and face the flag.

The Flag

The bald eagle is a very large bird with a white head. Bald eagles live in every state in United States of America except Hawaii. You can find a bald eagle on the back of a quarter and on a one dollar bill.

A bald eagle's wingspan can be six to eight feet. That's as big as two kids standing next to each other with their arms out, fingers touching.

Have you seen a bald eagle? Why do you think the bald bagle makes a good symbol for the United States of America?

The Bald Eagle

The Statue of Liberty stands on an island near New York City. She is one of the tallest statues in the world. She is made of copper and steel. She wears a long, flowing dress and carries a book and a torch.

Sometimes she is called "Lady Liberty." *Liberty* means freedom.

The Statue of Liberty was a gift from the people of France to the people of the United States on our country's 100th birthday.

The Statue of Liberty

American Symbols

Name: _____

We live in the United States of America.

①

The American flag has 13 red and white stripes and 50 white stars on a blue rectangle.

When you say the Pledge of Allegiance you are showing respect for the United States of America. You put your right hand over your heart, stand up straight, and face the flag.

The Bald Eagle is a symbol of America's freedom.

The Statue of Liberty is in New York. She is also a symbol of the United States of America.

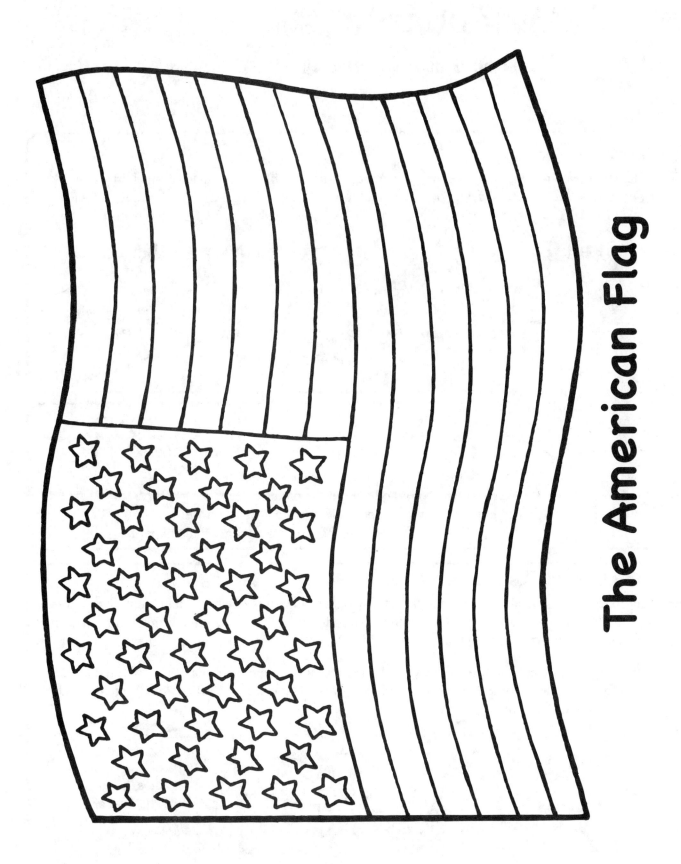

The American Flag

My Country *(cont)*

◉ Small Group Activities ◉

Civics

Patriotic Snack

Celebrate the colors of America by making a red, white, and blue fruit salad of blueberries, strawberries, and banana slices. For a math patterning activity, poke a hole in the center of each piece of fruit. Give each student a thin coffee stirrer and help skewer the fruit in a pattern.

You will need blueberries, strawberries, bananas, and/or coffee stirrers for this activity.

You will need crayons, glue, and brown paper lunch sacks for this activity. Brown feathers can also be added.

Bald Eagle Bag Puppet

Copy the patterns (page 195) for each student. Have students color and cut out the pattern pieces and glue them onto a paper bag to make a Bald Eagle puppet. Add brown feathers or color them on the paper bags.

Lady Liberty Costume

Headband: Cut a U-shaped opening in a sturdy paper plate (this is where the plate will slip over the child's head). Cut seven triangles from construction paper and glue them around the rim of the headband. Paint the headband green and, if desired, sprinkle on gold or silver glitter.

Torch: Cut triangular shapes into the end of an empty toilet paper roll. Paint the roll green and sprinkle with glitter. Gather red, orange, and yellow tissue paper and stuff or glue it into the end of the roll to create the flame.

Citizenship

You will need sturdy paper plates, a stapler, construction paper or tag board, empty toilet paper rolls, and red, orange, and yellow tissue paper for this activity.

Bald Eagle

Our Earth

◉ **Community Circle Activities** ◉

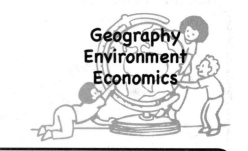
Nature Observation Walk

Take students on a walk through your campus or your neighborhood to observe nature. Before you go, talk with students about the difference between natural and man-made. Give examples: buildings, sidewalks, streets, and cars are man-made. Trees, plants, animals, air, and sunlight are natural. Tell students that they should look for as many natural things as they can find on your walk. If students are developmentally ready, provide notebooks or paper and pencils so students can record their observations.

When you return to the classroom, create a chart titled, "Our Natural World" and record anything students saw on the walk that was natural. Have students draw pictures and write or dictate about what they saw. Gather their pages into a book about "Our Natural World."

Natural Resources

Building on Where Does it Come From? (page 157), talk with students about natural resources. Natural resources are things in nature like air, water, and trees that we use to fill our wants and needs. Show students the Natural Resources mini posters on pages 197–199 and read the text aloud. Invite students to ask questions and discuss each natural resource. Ask students for examples of how they use each resource.

Natural Resources Song

Copy and display the mini poster on page 200 and sing The Natural Resources song with students.

Identifying Natural Resources

Use the worksheet on page 201 to help students identify some of the ways in which they use natural resources.

We need to breathe clean air to be healthy. Take a deep breath. Do you feel the air going into your lungs? Blow on your hand. Do you feel the air coming out of your mouth? Plants and animals also need air.

We cannot make air. Air is part of the Earth. Air is a natural resource.

Water

Our bodies need clean water to be healthy. We also use water to cook and to clean. What are some ways you use water?

We cannot make water. Water is part of the Earth. Water is a natural resource.

Trees

Trees give us many things. Some trees give us fruit, like apples and oranges. Some trees make homes for animals, like birds and squirrels.

Some trees we cut down and turn into wood and paper. Wood is used to make things like houses and furniture. Can you name some things made of wood?

Wood is also used to make paper. Can you name some things made from paper?

We cannot make trees, but we can plant them and take care of them as they grow. Trees are a natural resource.

⚙ The Natural Resource Song ⚙

(Sing to the tune of "The Wheels on the Bus.")

Oh, we need air to breathe every day
Every day, every day
Oh, we need air to breathe every day
Air is a natural resource.

Oh, we need water to drink and bathe
Drink and bathe, drink and bathe
Oh, we need water to drink and bathe
Water is a natural resource.

Oh, trees give us both paper and wood
Paper and wood, paper and wood
Oh, trees give us both paper and wood
Trees are a natural resource.

Directions: If the picture shows someone using water, circle the water drops. If the picture shows someone using trees, circle the tree.

Our Earth *(cont.)*

◎ **Community Circle Activities** ◎

**Economics
Environment**

Recycling

Before beginning this activity, break play dough into enough small chunks for each student to have one. You will find a recipe for play dough on page 208. Label a large box "Paper Recycling."

Give each student a small chunk of play dough. Ask students to make a shape, any shape with the dough. Then ask them to squash the shape and make another one. Ask them to squash that shape and make one last shape. Explain to students that what they are doing is called recycling, which means using the same material over and over again to make things.

Show students a sheet of used or scrap paper that is no longer needed. Explain that paper comes from trees, which are a natural resource. When we are finished with something made of paper and we no longer need it, we can recycle it. Show students the "Paper Recycling" box and place the paper into it. Tell students that the paper they are finished with will be taken to a place where the paper will be torn into little pieces and mixed with other paper and water to make new paper. So this piece of paper might be changed into a paper bag or a book. That way, we don't need to cut down more trees to make more paper.

Show students an aluminum can and a glass bottle. Explain that each of these can also be recycled. Aluminum cans can be melted and made into new cans. Glass bottles can be broken and melted and made into new bottles, just like when they squashed and reformed their play dough. If desired, place "Aluminum Recycling" and "Glass Recycling" boxes in the classroom as well.

You will need play dough, a box, scrap paper, an aluminum can, and a glass bottle for this activity.

Caring for the Earth

Copy and assemble the We Can Take Care of Our Earth minibook on pages 203–205 for each student.

Give each student a copy and let them color the pictures. Read the book with students following along in their own copies. Discuss each page.

Responsibility & Citizenship

We Can Take Care of Our Earth

Name: _____

We can help keep our Earth healthy and clean. We can put our trash in a trash can.

We can help keep our air clean. We can walk or ride our bikes.

We can help save trees. We can use less paper. We can recycle.

We can save water. We can turn the water off while we brush our teeth.

We can save energy. We can turn off the lights when we leave a room.

Our Earth (cont.)

Economics Environment

◉ Community Circle Activities ◉

Make Less Trash

Set a large box or bin out at snack or lunch time and ask students to put all of their trash in the box.

After lunch or snack, gather students around the box and look inside. As you pull out each item, have the students decide if it could be recycled or used again. Talk about how students could make less trash by bringing their food in reusable containers:

- thermoses or washable sports bottles instead of juice boxes, disposable water bottles, or cans

- washable plastic containers instead of plastic bags

- washable silverware instead of plastic

- lunch boxes instead of paper bags

Rinse any dirty items and keep all of the trash in the box. The next week, put out a new box and repeat the experience. Help students compare the amount of trash created—did they do better at creating less trash?

Don't Be a Litterbug

Give each student a bag and some disposable gloves. Go out on the playground, around campus or the neighborhood, or to a local park and collect litter. Bring the bags of litter back to the classroom and look at what students found. Ask students:

- What might happen if an animal ate some of this litter?

- Will these things help the plants and trees grow?

- What would happen to these things if it rained and they washed down the storm drains?

- Can any of this be recycled?

- Let students decorate recycled paper grocery sacks to make litter bags for their cars or homes.

The Litter Song

Try to sing to the tune of "She'll Be Coming Round the Mountain"

If you see a piece of litter, pick it up.
If you see a piece of litter, pick it up.
If you see a piece of litter,
please put it in a trash can.
If you see a piece of litter, pick it up.

Graphing Directions

Create a class graph using a pocket chart. Place cards across the bottom of the pocket chart to create columns or down the left side of the pocket chart to create rows (see illustrations). Make a name card for each student to place on the graph—you can even add a photograph. It helps students read the graph if the row/column heading cards are a different color than the students' name cards. If you do not have a pocket chart, draw a graph on chart paper and let students use sticky notes for their names. The vertical arrangement is usually better for graphs with fewer columns and the horizontal rows work well when there are many choices. Don't forget to add a title at the top of your graph. Read the graph title to students and have them place their name cards in the appropriate column or row.

The most important part of any graphing activity is analyzing the results. Help students "read" each column or row; "Two people ride in a car to school, five people take the bus, and three people walk to school." Then compare the columns, "More people like the color blue than the color pink," "Red and purple are the colors that the most people like." You can cut out and use the Sample Graph Analysis Questions card to help you lead students in analyzing graphs.

Sample Graph Analysis Questions

What is this graph about?

How many students chose _____?

Which column/row has the most?

Which was second?   How many picked that one?

How many more students chose _____ than _____?

Which row/column had the least?

How many fewer students chose _____ than _____?

Play Dough Recipe

Ingredients

1 cup flour

1 cup water

$\frac{1}{2}$ cup salt

1 Tablespoon cooking oil

1 Tablespoon cream of tartar

1 package unsweetened powdered drink mix (for color and scent)

Mix all of the ingredients in a non-stick skillet. Cook on medium heat, stirring constantly. Cook until the dough pulls away from the pan and forms a ball. Let it cool a bit, and then knead well. Store the dough in an airtight container or resealable bag.